"It's a Jungle Out There!"

RON SNELL

Book One of the Rani Adventures

Copyright Ron Snell
FIRST EDITION PRINTED June, 1995
ISBN 0-929292-83-9
Library of Congress 95-076626
ALL RIGHTS RESERVED
Printed in the United States of America by Lithocolor Press, Inc.
Cover by Cyndi Allison
(Use coupons in back to order extra copies of this and
other books from HANNIBAL BOOKS)

DEDICATION

When I started writing this book, I never dreamed how much more I would come to understand and appreciate my parents. Their commitment to God took us to the middle of nowhere, and their trust allowed us to take advantage of all the jungle and the Machiguengas had to offer.

I'm proud to dedicate this book to Dad and Mom, with my gratitude and love.

ACKNOWLEDGEMENTS

I'd love to take all of the credit and blame for this book myself. Unfortunately, my mother and father, brother and sisters and wife are sure to read it, and they all know good and well that they had a major part in supplying information, editing for accuracy and arguing about whose memory is best. I'm glad to share a lot of the blame and a little of the credit with all of them.

Once we settled our differences long enough for me to get the stories on paper, Marti Hefley of HANNIBAL BOOKS made sure the writing wouldn't embarrass them or me forever. For example, she took out my comment about being "barely conceived" in the jungle, noting that you're never "barely conceived." There, I got it in after all.

Cyndi Allison made sure that no matter what the inside of the book might be like, the cover, front and back, would be beautiful.

Beyond those key helpers, I've had special people along the way who have urged me to put my unusual life on paper. I hope they don't regret it.

My thanks to each of you!

Table of Contents

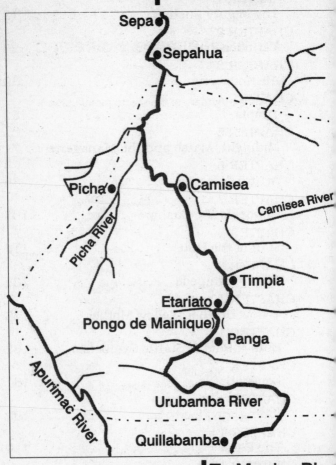

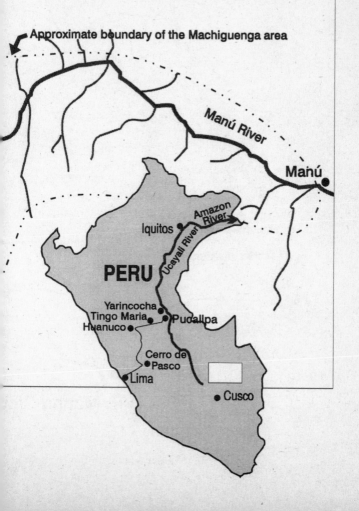

The Machiguenga Homeland

Approximate boundary of the Machiguenga area

Manú River

Manú

Amazon River

Iquitos

Ucayali River

PERU

Yarincocha
Tingo Maria
Huanuco
Pucallpa

Cerro de Pasco

Lima

Cusco

"Tell us all about your life in the jungle," they asked me again and again.

"I don't think I can," I answered. "It was such a different world — how can I possibly explain it?"

"Well then," said a soft-spoken little friend in the front row, "just tell us some stories."

And so I did. Some were funny, some were sad, and some were ... well ... you'll see.

CHAPTER 1

The Mighty Push

My brother Terry and I were sitting on our front porch carving balsa wood and our fingers into bloody canoes and airplanes when Dad hollered at us. Dad's normal volume was holler or higher.

"Rani! Teri!" He used the Machiguenga version of Ronny and Terry. "How about if you two help Arturo get back home?" As usual, it sounded more like a Navy gunner's order than a question, but we jumped at the chance for an adventure.

"Sure," we stereo'd, wiping the blood off our jack knives. "How'd he get down here?" Arturo's house was two hours and two rapids upriver from Camisea, a small village of about twenty huts deep in the jungle of Southern Peru. We lived there off and on as our parents helped the Machiguengas with community development projects and worked to translate the New Testament into their language.

"I brought Apa's canoe down." Arturo answered in Machiguenga, smiling because he'd figured out our English question. Of course since "Apa" means "Father," and since a Machiguenga calls just about every man a generation up "Apa," we hadn't the slightest idea who he was talking about.

"I have to take it back up to him, but there'll be some other canoe you can borrow to come back in." We knew he didn't have any idea if there would or wouldn't be a canoe we could borrow or how we'd get back home, but at the time it didn't seem to matter, even though I was just nine and Terry ten.

Besides, we liked Arturo, our "big brother" according to the Machiguengas who had adopted us into their big family. He was a young bilingual school teacher with a squinty-eyed smile, an enviable gold canine tooth, a couple of railroad track tattooes running across his cheeks and an unconscious habit of going "kmh" through his beaky nose.

"You need to get going right away so you can be back by dark," Dad told us. Every once in a while he sounded as if he cared whether or not we survived these trips. "Grab some lunch and some extra water." We joined Arturo at the table.

Lunch was fast, but not fast enough to escape Mom's collection of practical suggestions. She obviously cared a lot whether we survived this adventure. In between swallows of boiled water and smoked monkey meat we nodded and shook our crew cut blonde heads to indicate that yes, we would be careful. No, we would not let ourselves get sunburned. Yes, we would find a canoe to come home in. No, we would not drink the river water unless we were drowning in it.

Lunch gulped and instructions endured, Terry grabbed a paddle and the three of us

hurried barefoot down our short path to the
river. Apa's canoe was pulled up on the
mucky bank, tied with a vine to make sure
it wouldn't escape while no one was looking.
Canoes are precious, since it takes about six
months to make one.

Arturo got in the front, Terry in the
middle, and I in the back. That made Terry
and Arturo the standing polers and me the
sitting paddler. We were all stripped down
to gym shorts.

Now you have to understand that poling
a dugout against a strong current is hard
work. One reason is that you have to stand
up to do it. Apa's canoe was twenty-six feet
long, round and only twenty inches wide. It
was hacked out of a tree and still looked a
lot like one. About the only thing that made
this canoe stable was practice, which Terry
and I'd been getting since we were born.

Another thing that makes poling hard is
that you have to push on the pole with just
the right parts of your body. It's difficult to
describe which ones those are because we
kind of grew up doing it.

Suffice it to say that when inexperienced
visitors tried it, they didn't pole with the
right parts of their bodies. Every time their
poles slipped or stuck in the mud they put

on a gymnastics performance. Head first, feet kicking, spraddle-legged, flap-armed and open-mouthed they'd fly into the river. Machiguengas loved to watch outsiders try to pole, as long as they weren't in the canoe.

Arturo and Terry and I had it pretty easy for the first twenty minutes. The current was sluggish and the water clear. Three feet down we could just make out the stingrays camouflaged in their mudbeds and sucker fish leaving pale white circles where they'd sucked the moss off the rocks.

I love watching Machiguengas pole their canoes: the near liquid grace of muscles flowing and bulging, the rhythmic rise and fall of the bow, the seemingly effortless balancing act, the hearty and hilarious grunts when the going gets tough. The tougher it gets, the more the Machis laugh.

"We need to get over on the left side, Rani." Arturo reminded me as we approached our first rapid. There we could edge against the side of a rock cliff and take advantage of whirlpools and backwaters as we inched our way upstream. The current was roaring now. I could see the muscles in Arturo's bare back and shoulders flow and bulge under the increasing strain. Terry and he were taking turns, one planting his pole before the other moved his. That kept us from slipping back downriver. It was my job to keep the boat pointed exactly into the current and close to the bank.

We inched our way slowly, steadily, carefully through the eddies, backwaters and burbles, ever closer to the big waves, until we could go no further and it was all Arturo and Terry could do to just keep us where we were.

"It's getting too swift on this side, Rani. Let's cross," Arturo commanded, and in a flash he pushed the nose out into the current.

"Eheh," (Machiguenga for "uhuh"), I answered, and exploded into action. With my arms breaking and my heart pounding I thrashed my paddle like a wild banshee. It was all up to me, because I was the only one with a paddle.

Machiguenga paddles sometimes need a lot of thrashing because they aren't much more than a stick with one flat side and a handle on it. The handle is so you can tell which end to put in the water.

Lots of times the biggest difference between a pole and a paddle is how long it is. Poles have to reach the bottom of the river. Paddles only have to reach the water line, which is often about even with the sides of the canoe. That's when bailing gourds come in handy.

I knew that crossing the swift river we'd have to be quick. Otherwise the canoe would race backwards down the river faster than it was creeping across the river. We'd end up so far back downriver that there wouldn't be any good poling and we'd have to come right back across. If that happened, it would be quiet for a long time. Unless, of course, someone fell in or got hurt in the process. Then the others would laugh their heads off.

Well, we only lost thirty feet before Terry and Arturo found the bottom with their poles. Not bad. We edged up to the rapid from the other side, leaped out of the canoe at just the right moment, and began dragging it through the boulders and waves.

Since we were barefooted, our feet crunched down between the rocks and our toes got twisted and our toenails broken. The water grabbed at our legs, always trying to wash them out from under us. We took turns slipping and falling and frantically grabbing the canoe for support until we could get up and help pull some more. I reckon that was about as much fun as two boys could ever have in this life.

Our legs got banged and our feet got cut and we pushed and strained and pulled for fifteen minutes until finally, slowly we hauled our heavy canoe into the smooth water at the top of the rapid. Panting, we tumbled in. Grabbed poles and paddle. Breathed easy for a couple of minutes even as we worked to keep the canoe from going backwards right back down the rapid.

Arturo kind of laughed as if we were the best entertainment he'd had in a long time and went "kmh" a couple of times and we were off again. We'd made it half way in a little over an hour. Not bad.

The second rapid wasn't as difficult as the first, and then a long straight stretch of relative calm brought a row of thatched huts into view. Worn paths tied the houses to the sandbar between them and the river. Butterflies and other flies swarmed around piles of dog poop in the sand. Picturesque.

A few naked children splashed in the water, but as far as we could see, there were no canoes beached on the sand. We should have known the men would be out hunting and the women would be at their gardens.

"I'm going," Arturo told Terry, and then

me. Culturally, he had to say it to each of us.

"You're going," we both responded automatically. In Machiguenga, farewells are a short statement of the obvious. We were on our own.

The village, as far as we could tell, was virtually deserted. We had lived there a couple of years before and knew almost everyone who wasn't home. The few old women we found in smoke filled cookhouses didn't know anything about canoes.

"Let's just swim back," Terry suggested after all other possibilities had faded. To us it seemed a brilliant solution, though one that no Machiguenga would have considered in a thousand years.

Machiguenga adults don't swim just for the fun of it. To them a river is a faucet, a laundromat, a fish market, a highway, a bathtub and a toilet. Not necessarily in that order, unfortunately. Only to us white outsiders was it a fabulous swimming hole.

We headed out across the blinding white sandbar, through the rainbow clouds of butterflies. At one spot, just before we reached the shoreline, forty of fifty of them swarmed together in a brilliant splotch of yellow-orange. I found them irrestible.

Raised our paddle high in the air. Smacked it down on the butterflies with a mighty WHOP! Missed the butterflies, hit the poop, broke the paddle.

Now we not only had nothing to paddle, but nothing to paddle it with. For some reason that seemed worse, and Terry let me know it.

"Why'd you do that? You don't ever, ever, ever whop things with your paddle. Especially things that are swarming on a pile of dog poop. Now what are we going to do?"

There wasn't much we could do, so we pitched the paddle parts, waded into the river and swam to the other side. Swam, in fact, right into the perfect solution to our problem: a log left over from the last high water. It wasn't much of a log as Amazonian logs go, but we were in no position to be choosy and this one at least looked as if it might barely keep two little boys afloat if we could launch it and stay on it.

"Push!"

"I am pushing."

"Push harder and pick up on it while you're pushing!"

"I am pushing harder and if I try to lift it I just sink into the mud."

We heaved and ho'd and grunted and strained like a couple of skinny mud wrestlers until finally the log oozed itself off the bank into the current. Then we scrambled aboard bareback and locked our legs around it like parenthetical clamps. Across the river, Machiguenga kids silently stared like now they'd seen it all.

Right then a canoe materialized out of nowhere, with a frowning paddler at the stern. The Machiguengas had always taken such good care of us that since we were babies our parents had let us go anywhere with them. Now one of our very concerned "fathers" offered to take us home, even though it would mean an overnight in Camisea for him.

"No thanks," we said. "We're okay and we have a log to get home on." He wasn't impressed, well aware that a log wasn't the same as a canoe, even if both came from trees. Eventually we convinced him that we'd be fine, and we drifted slowly away as he sat in his canoe, typically not showing any hint of how stupid he thought we were.

Now remember, we didn't have any way to steer our log. You don't really steer logs anyway. Steering a log in a river is kind of like steering a buffalo in a stampede. When you're riding a log, the log chooses the route, which is exhilirating until it decides to grind your legs off against a cliff or roll over in a rapid.

All of that seemed unlikely as we started off. For a nine year old, there isn't much to match riding your very own log down a cool clear river in the middle of the jungle with your big brother. Towering trees dripped green vines into the water. The occasional pair of macaws raaawwkk-ed their way across our narrow window of blue sky. As we approached the first rapid, our speed picked up to an exhilarating pace.

A frightening pace, to be exact. Being totally out of control added to the thrill, and we both screened our fears behind screams of enthusiasm as we lifted our legs, dug in our fingernails and balanced for dear life.

"If this thing turns sideways, jump off," Terry yelled. Running sideways, the log could catch on a rock, buck us off downriver and then pancake us on it's way past.

Boulders raced past us. Waves splashed and submerged us. We shot right through a forked tree branch that stuck up at the waterline and we dodged the branches so they wouldn't scrape us off. Beneath us we could hear the crunchy sound of rocks grinding each other into sand and briefly considered what that might feel like. Our log flew straight as an arrow past the rock bar, did a couple of spins in the whirlpools and eddies, bumped into a cliff or two, and finally slowed to a casual drift.

"Wow," I shouted, "that was great!"

"We're just lucky we didn't get killed," Terry answered. "I don't know how we're going to get through the next one."

In the lazy, slow section between rapids we could relax. We took turns throwing rocks at the kingfishers, jumping into the river, diving to the bottom, and sprawling turtle-like on the log to warm ourselves. Then, as the afternoon wore dangerously on, the roar of the second, worse rapid filled our nervous ears.

If our log just chose its own route, it would snuggle up to the right bank and follow the current through a hard right turn. That turn would end us up in a high speed, battering-ram approach to a log jam before we swung into a hard left turn that would run us through some ominously high waves.

None of that sounded fun, so with adrenalized energy we hand paddled the log to a vine-covered mud bank for a reconnoiter just above the rapid. Terry's confident opinion was that he should point the front of the log out into the water and I should give us such a mighty push that our momentum would carry us twenty feet to the left side of the channel before the current could crush us against the right side.

There was clearly one pivotal point on which this plan would succeed or fail: *the mighty push*. Terry repeated that three or four times, louder each time, as if sheer volume would overcome the roar of the river and the inherent difficulties in pulling off such a maneuver.

Ready or not, the front of the log swung briefly in the right direction. I grunted, strained, heaved and shoved as mighty a push as I'd ever pushed. The log didn't notice. Mostly my legs went deep into the mud, so that as the current caught the log and raced off with it, I had the horrible feeling that I was going to get left behind. Frantic, I worked my legs loose from the mud, swam like fury and caught up just in time.

Terry was yelling about my specific and general failures, the rapids were roaring with laughter and I was trying to get back on board in the few seconds of life I had left.

In those brief seconds, we made the dreaded sharp right turn, shot down the shallow introductory section and crashed into accumulated debris along the bank. We had one more chance at life.

"Push," Terry yelled, and I pushed as I've never pushed anything before or since. "We've got to get to the left of those waves." As if I didn't know it already.

This time my push did a little good. Our momentum carried us ten feet across the channel before we spun around, submarined backwards just along the sides of the biggest waves, and ejected ourselves from the log before it killed us. We hit the backwaters and whirlpools swimming for our lives and having a pretty one-sided conversation about the "mighty push." Fortunately I couldn't hear most of what Terry was saying.

We never got back on the log. The rest of the way home we swam, walked along muddy banks, watched the birds fly home to bed and jabbed at stingrays with sharp sticks just to relieve the boredom.

It was nearly dark by the time we limped back up the path toward the light of the Coleman lantern in our house.

"Have a good trip?" Dad asked.

"Yeah — great!" we said.

"How'd you get home?" asked Mom more specifically.

"We're starving," we answered. I wonder if she ever found out.

CHAPTER 2

Yarinacocha

And then there was the time — well, I suppose I should back up a bit. After all, I wasn't born on a log in the Camisea. The story of how I got there is as interesting as the ride itself. It all began when I was conceived in the jungle within a couple weeks of my parents' arrival in Peru.

I can't be more specific about the timing because they won't. Still, I'm terribly proud of my rainforest roots even though I didn't have a thing to do with it. It was a close call: Two weeks after I became me, Dad and Mom returned to Lima to study Spanish.

"You may have been ... uhhhhhh ... conceived in the green jungle," Mom once told me with just a bit of bashful modesty, "but you developed on green apples in Lima."

The green apples kept Mom and therefore me alive long enough to be born. Within weeks of my birth, we were on our way back to the jungle. More specifically, we were on our way to Pucallpa and Yarinacocha, two places that were even more obscure than they sound.

Faucett Airlines had a bi-weekly flight to Pucallpa. Not that it always made it, but at least it was scheduled. We boarded a DC-3 for what we hoped would be a successful flight over the Andes.

The DC-3 couldn't quite make it over the tops of the highest mountains, so it had to fly through a lower pass. Frequently the pass was filled with clouds, forcing a return to Lima and a re-try the next day. Sometimes passengers had to try four or five days in a row before they finally made it through to the jungle. The only alternative was a five hundred mile one lane road that only a drunk trucker would travel. A drunk trucker or my Dad, but that's another story.

The climb out of Lima was breathtaking. Literally. Within a few minutes everyone on board had a clear plastic umbilical cord blowing oxygen into his mouth or nose, the only way to keep passengers from passing out at 16,000 feet in the unpressurized cabin.

Luckily for us, the pass was clear on our first try and the landing in Tingo Maria for more fuel was routine. In the air again, we flew northeast through the mountains. Then, as abruptly as they had reared up, the mountains fell away, sinking into an endless ocean of deep green jungle dotted here and there with the exceptional red or yellow tree.

"You can put your oxygen tubes away now," the flight attendant announced in Spanish. Eardrums popped the other direction and the cabin temperature began to climb tropically. We were going down.

Pucallpa's airstrip didn't exactly inspire confidence. It was made of red clay that swelled and shrank in the alternating heat and rain. That made for mud sometimes, dust sometimes, and bumps all the time.

Then of course there were always pigs on the runway, wallowing in the mudholes. And dogs fighting over scraps. That meant the pilot had to buzz the strip three or four times to scare the animals away and then land before they decided it was safe to come back.

In spite of the obstacles, our highly skilled pilot performed his bi-weekly miracle once again and got us safely on the ground, around the mudholes and stopped before the end of the runway. Dad and Mom clambered out into a dank, musty humidity each carrying a baby boy.

"Hey, welcome to Pucallpa! How was the flight?" It was Uncle Les Bancroft's job to meet the plane this week. He wasn't really our uncle, but we called every adult we knew "aunt" or "uncle" to show respect and to make up for the fact that we didn't even know our real aunts and uncles.

"Well, let's get your bags and then we'll get on out to Yarinacocha." Uncle Les and Dad hoisted us into the truck.

A fifteen-second look at Pucallpa was enough to make anyone wonder why they had just risked their lives to get there. It was a ramshackle clapboard frontier town of two thousand people, two Jeeps and two stores built on red clay beside the mighty Ucayali River. Feet, bicycles and horses got people around town.

Two arteries pumped life into Pucallpa: the first was the Ucayali itself, connecting Peru to Brazil via the Amazon River. Boats could bring raw materials from upriver and goods from downriver. The second artery was the winding, rutted road connecting it to Lima. Trucks carried the raw materials to Lima and returned with frontier essentials.

"Are you all set?" The five mile trip from Pucallpa to Yarinacocha could easily take three hours, so Uncle Les was eager to start back.

A rutted, undrained road had been hacked out of the jungle by early pioneers. Then they acquired a military surplus Burma Jeep to drive over it. The Burma Jeep was more a monstrous primeval green mutant pickup truck than a Jeep. It was designed to knock down trees, stop marauding elephants and transport soldiers with no nerves in their butts.

With its high clearance and massive winch the Burma Jeep could go most anywhere. Passengers sat on hard wooden fold-down benches that ran the length of the uncovered bed. There was little to hold onto except each other and the luggage. The transmission, lacking synchro-mesh gears, growled angrily every time Uncle Les tried to shift. After an hour we passed an enormous tree that towered over the road.

"We're halfway," Uncle Les shouted as if going three miles in an hour were excellent progress. "That tree is our marker." Only two and a half miles to go.

An hour later, covered with dust and bruised from top to bottom, mainly bottom, we reached Yarinacocha. The small cluster of clapboard houses perched on the high bank of a ten-mile long oxbow lake formed when the Ucayali River changed course. Peru's Ministry of Education had given the land to the Summer Institute of Linguistics (SIL), a sister organization to Wycliffe Bible Translators, to be used as a headquarters for educational work in the jungle.

We broke out onto the lake and ground up a long hill to the main building on the center. Sandaled colleagues in rumpled clothes came running when they heard the Burma Jeep come in.

"Welcome to Yarinacocha. Great to have you back. Did you bring the mail from

Lima?" It was clear they cared more about the mail than us. Smiles, jokes, renewed friendships and camaraderie all around as strong arms lowered Mom and Terry and me to the unbouncing ground.

We were all slathered with bug repellent to keep from being consumed by chiggers. The repellent helped a lot, but even so one of the first things any new arrival had to learn was how to scratch pretty personal places without looking like they were scratching. Some people got so good at it that we all just thought they were dancing to some strange tribal music.

After unpacking the essentials in a one room thatched house, we joined the hardy gang for a group swim in the lake, the only place to bathe, and supper in the common dining hall, the only place to eat. Then, totally done in, we probed our way by flashlight to bed.

We had come home. Home to howler monkeys, cicadas, mangoes, tarantulas, mosquitos, tin roofs, screen windows, outhouses, bananas, orchids and piranhas.

That first night, as owls hoo-hoo-hooted and giant rhinocerous beetles banged into the screens and hopeful frogs croaked seductively to their mates, Dad and Mom paused to thank God for the privilege of finally being on the edge of nowhere, on their way to the middle of nowhere. My life, at six weeks of age, had come full circle.

I learned to crawl on our mahogany floor while Dad and Mom tried to figure out which tribe they would translate the Bible for. That wasn't quite as simple as it sounds, since no one quite knew what tribes were out there. Uncle Cam Townsend, the founder and director of Wycliffe Bible Translators and SIL, had already recruited Dad to do some pretty hairy work trying to sort it all out.

"Wayne, we need someone to go exploring for us. Would you spend some time finding out who's out there in the jungle and whether or not we could work with them?" Never mind that some of those unknown tribal groups were inclined to kill outsiders.

By the time Dad had wandered the jungle by airplane, canoe and trail, and had spent nights running away from hostile Indians who presumably didn't want him to work there, his list of possible tribes included the Shimacu, Aguaruna, Huitoto, and Orejon.

Once the list of tribal names started to

grow, SIL teams chose which ones they'd like to work with.

"We'd like the Shimacu," Dad and Mom ventured.

"Well, I really kind of had my heart set on them," someone else answered.

"All right then, we'll work with the Huitoto's."

"I think the Lord is directing us to work with them," said another team with a stronger sense of guidance.

Whenever the Machiguengas came up, my folks said no thanks, they weren't interested. But of course they said they would pray about it because even if you're not at all jazzed about something, when you're a missionary you have to say you'll pray about it. Eventually the Machiguengas were about the only ones left, so Dad and Mom became their linguists. We've never been sorry.

CHAPTER 3

Air Knockers

Soon Dad was off to find the Machiguengas, and he ended up at Timpia, which was about as far from anywhere as you can get. If you've ever heard of Timpia, you're either an avid reader of National Geographic, an intrepid Urubamba river explorer or a friend of ours.

Timpia was a pain to get to. It definitely wasn't on the way from anywhere to anywhere else. It's two thatched houses were perched on a high bank over the

Timpia River near where it emptied into the Urubamba River, one of the fast flowing tributaries of the Ucayali River and eventually the Amazon.

Floating north down the Urubamba to Timpia from the ancient ruins of Machu Picchu and Quillabamba was next to impossible, although a few Machiguengas tried it and some even survived to tell about it. The main obstacle was a treacherous gorge full of foaming white rapids, spinning whirlpools and swirling cross currents. Balsa rafts could come down it with a moderate chance of not doing cartwheels or shattering into toothpicks, but it wasn't something you'd want to do very often. Dugout canoes were even riskier.

Getting 500 miles upriver to Timpia by boat from Pucallpa, the closest real town downriver, was certainly possible if you had half a lifetime to do it. Few people wanted to get there that badly.

Fortunately, by the time Dad went to Timpia, SIL had an Aeronca float plane that could fly him the whole way there. All the Indians fled into the jungle when the plane pulled up to the bank, but one tall, skinny man with a drooping black mustache came to greet Dad.

"*Buenos dias.* Walter Snell *a sus ordenes.*" Dad stuck out his hand and used his middle name because 'Wayne' sounds like 'whiney' when you say it in Spanish.

"Juan Mendoza. *Mucho gusto. Bienvenido a Timpia.*" It turned out he was a very bright Spaniard with an engineering degree from Harvard, far removed from his native land. Apparently he had gotten into some sort of political trouble in Spain and had exiled himself to Peru, ending up in Timpia, of all places.

"Who all lives here?" Dad wanted to know. There were only two houses in the small clearing and it seemed an unlikely place to meet a Spaniard.

"There are about a dozen adults that all live in that one big house, plus all of their children," Don Juan answered. "They work for me clearing land and planting crops."

"What kind of stuff do you grow?"

"Mostly rice and a poisonous plant they use downriver to manufacture insecticides. I don't make a lot of money from it, but it's a living, and I don't need much money out here." He smiled as he glanced around at the surrounding jungle, hundreds of miles from any stores.

After the small talk was over, Dad came

to the real point of his visit.

"My wife and I would like to learn Machiguenga. Where do you think would be the best place for us to live while we're doing that?" Legally Don Juan didn't own the area, but he knew a lot about the Machiguengas. It wouldn't have been smart to just barge in.

"Oh, please come and live here in Timpia. You're welcome to build your own house and bring your family. I'd be happy to have your company here and help you in any way I can." What he meant was that he'd be thrilled to talk to someone who had heard of Spain and Harvard.

Timpia seemed like an awfully small place to begin working, but it was as large a community as the Machiguengas had. So, wanting to capitalize on the warm welcome, Dad flew back out in November to build us a house. Before he left he loaded bulky equipment, including a kerosene refrigerator for my milk, a hand-cranked washing machine for my diapers and a hand-cranked sewing machine, on a motor launch. The launch would take it to Atalaya, about halfway by river. From there a small plane could pick it up and transfer it to Timpia someday. That process took a full five months.

On Don Juan's orders, the Indians had already cleared a spot for our new house by the time Dad got there. It sat on a hill high above the river, close to the foothills of the Andes mountains, with fabulous views of both the sunrise and the sunset. Our first tribal home would be one of the most beautiful in the jungle.

Dad stayed there five weeks. When he came home, he had lost 35 pounds and gained a beard, plus amoeba and a few other intestinal parasites.

In April, it was our turn. Colleagues huddled on the bank to pray as Mom contemplated six months of isolation with two little boys. Dad had once again gone out ahead of us, so it was just Mom, Terry, me and the pilot in the little Aeronca airplane, affectionately known as an "air knocker," or "knocker" for short.

Knockers were canvas-covered planes designed to fly with more or less a 440 pound load. SIL's knockers were on floats, which made it pretty difficult to get a full load into the air.

Suction between the water and the floats kept the plane from getting up on step, or planing, and the only way to break the suction was to rock the plane forward and backwards.

Sometimes the pilot tried to get one float out of the water before the other. Divide and conquer. Push the stick in and out and turn it. If the plane didn't get off before the engine overheated or it ran out of room, the pilot slowed back down, turned around, rested a few minutes and tried again. In later years I thought that was the most fun of the whole trip, and I was always a bit disappointed when we finally succeeded.

Pilots differed in their ability to get Knockers off the water. One pilot whose name I won't mention often roared back and forth, back and forth until eventually he had used up enough fuel to lighten the load and get airborne. By then he sometimes didn't have enough to get where he was going.

I don't remember our first trip to Timpia, but I do remember many just like it. Uncle Jim Price was our pilot. Eccentric, adventuresome, fun-loving Uncle Jim with bare feet and tattered trousers and a stained T-shirt and unruly hair. He was a jack-of-all-trades and master of most.

Uncle Jim loved Aeroncas and could make them do everything but fetch and roll over. Maybe he could even make them roll over, but if so he never told anyone. It wouldn't have been well received by our aviation administrators. He certainly never rolled an Aeronca while my mother was on board. She would have strangled him with his seat belt.

Folklore has it that Uncle Jim once landed an Aeronca on Lake Yarinacocha with so little fuel that it ran out before he could taxi in. Swimming spectators watched him calmly paddle it home. I think he finally quit flying when they started making rules about safety.

In spite of Uncle Jim's expertise and our colleagues' prayers, it still took three tries to get us off the lake at Yarinacocha, since we were loaded to the max. We were always loaded to the max.

In this case, our load included two fully screened cribs for Terry and me, probably made out of mahogany because it was cheap and easy to get. We also had five-gallon cans of cookies and crackers, canned vegetables and fruit, baby formula, office supplies and reel to reel tape recorders for language study, boxes of medicine, a two-way radio about the size of an apartment refrigerator, a generator to run the radio and miscellaneous boxes and bags and bundles.

Roaring like a pride of lions, we finally lifted off and Mom waved good-bye to friends she didn't plan to see for six months. As usual there was no room for seats, so Mom sat on a lumpy green duffel bag and we sat on her. I don't remember if she was lumpy and green, but one can assume so given the turbulent tropical air.

It took five hours to get 350 air miles to Timpia. Aeroncas weren't particularly fast, and we had to stay in sight of the river's winding route in case engine trouble forced us back down on the water. In a float plane, being forced down on the river was a minor interruption. Being forced down anywhere else could ruin the whole trip.

The view from the little windows was of rivers and jungles and rivers and jungles and, for five hours, rivers and jungles. The Amazon rainforest stretched endlessly in every direction, an unbroken ocean of green broccoli splotched here and there with red or yellow. Once in a long while, a transluscent feather of smoke marked a tiny hut in a little clearing beside the river.

Our only stop was in Atalaya, a frontier military outpost where the Tambo and Urubamba rivers join to form the Ucayali.

Big launches could get that far upriver, carrying 55 gallon barrels of aviation fuel that they stockpiled on the bank. The men who helped Uncle Jim roll the barrels of gas down to the plane were quite captivated by the two little white boys who emerged for a wiggle. Mom understood enough Spanish by then to know that they were taking bets on how long our white skins would last when the river gnats attacked us in Timpia. It wasn't a reassuring conversation, and as it turned out, they had good reason to be concerned.

Taking off from a river was even more exciting than taking off the lake. Uncle Jim had to hand crank the propeller to start the engine, clamber along the slippery float without getting his head chopped off, squeeze into the cockpit, yell at his helpers to turn the plane and push it away from the bank, and hope that the engine didn't cut out before he took off. Sometimes it did, and he'd have to paddle like fury or scramble back to the front of a float for more cranking while the current carried the plane off downriver.

Of course it took a few tries again to get off the water after refueling in Atalaya. Mom rocked with the plane, subconsciously trying to help it, and we rocked with Mom, since we were still sitting on her.

Once back in the air, we turned further south and followed the Urubamba. Underneath us, the jungle got more and more interesting. At first little lumps, then genuine hills, and finally rugged bamboo covered cliffs and mountains broke up the landscape. The muddy beaches downriver gave way to sandy and rocky beaches upriver. Instead of endless clay banks, we flew over red cliffs cut bare by the rushing river. The Urubamba was clear and fast, instead of sluggish and brown.

Slowly we gained altitude as we approached the edge of the Andes and the mouth of the Timpia River, 1,450 feet above sea level. At last, Uncle Jim pointed out the tiny clearing in the middle of the endless jungle, and the grey-brown palm-leafed roof of the huge communal house where all the Machiguengas lived together. There was another house some distance away. That would be Don Juan's home. In between those two was the only other house in the area. It looked tiny from the air and still had a dark green roof of new leaves. Dad had just built it, for us.

We touched down and skipped along the

surface until Uncle Jim cut the engine, then taxied up beside dugout canoes tied to the bank where Dad and Don Juan were waiting with big smiles on their faces. Only a handful of men and boys were brave enough to join them beside the river. They weren't smiling.

Most of the welcoming party wore long coarse reddish brown "cushmas," robes made of homespun cotton. A couple had smudgy red paint on their faces. The men had what looked like headbands holding down neatly trimmed bangs that hung right down past their eyebrows, pretty much hiding their eyes in dark shadows. As it turned out the bangs were shiny black feathers that perfectly matched the Indians' hair.

Beyond the brave men and boys who risked their lives to meet us, more cautious men, women and children hid in the bushes and trees high on the bank, waiting to see what sort of aliens would climb out of the bright yellow UFO. To be on the safe side, they were ready to run for their lives.

Expectations of a fabulous show ran high, and no one was disappointed. When Mom handed Terry and me out the door of the plane, covert giggles and murmurs of wonder rippled through the bushes. Dad introduced each of us by pointing and saying our names. Mom was "Señora Beti." Terry was "Teri." I was, and forever remained, "Rani."

We and our considerable baggage were dumped on the rocky beach in front of our new home. Once unloaded, it took a lot of help to get us up the 100 foot bank that first time. Dad, scrambling for a footing in the loose shale, carried me. Victor, the head man of the small group of Machiguengas living there, awkwardly carried Terry. Victor clearly would have been more comfortable running up the steep, slippery bank with a 15 gallon barrel of kerosene on his shoulder. Little boys were for women to carry.

Watching Mom climb the bank, everyone wondered just what was wrong with her. She couldn't see obvious footholds, couldn't get any traction, couldn't make any progress even though she kept flopping around grabbing at things. It was pretty clear that if she didn't get some help, she'd spend the rest of her life on the rocky beach. Unfortunately it was totally inappropriate for a Machiguenga man to help her and the women were still hidden high in the bushes.

Finally Don Juan the gallant Spaniard came to her rescue. Pulling on one end and pushing on the other, he coaxed her thrashing legs slowly up the hill while everyone else ran past carrying our belongings and discreetly laughing.

The puzzled Machiguengas couldn't figure out why we were there. Nor could they understand how we would survive if we couldn't even get up the bank by ourselves or say anything intelligible. Oh well, for now it didn't really matter. This was going to be a great show!

CHAPTER 4

Timpia

Our first tribal home looked, felt and smelled like the inside of a rattan basket. The floor, two feet off the ground, bounced when we walked. There were cracks between the slats of the rough walls. The palm-leaf roof was neatly interlaced and tied. For the rest of my life, the smell of fresh cut palm leaves and split palm trunks would remind me of a new home.

Our floor bounced because it was made of pona. Pona came from a special kind of palm tree with a trunk about 14 inches in diameter. The outside of the trunk is tough as nails. Actually, tougher than nails, if you've ever tried to pound one into it. The inside is a fibrous spongy kind of stuff that's pretty easy to clean out.

To make a floor, the Machiguengas chopped down a pona palm and cut the trunk into sections about eight feet long. Longer sections would have been more convenient, but they weighed tons. Carrying them to a canoe and then from the canoe up the bank to the house was crunching hard work.

Now, just having chunks of trunks for a floor wouldn't be all that comfortable, so the next step was to make a full-length cut down one side sort of like cutting a hollow cardboard tube lengthwise. Of course a cardboard tube is easier to flatten out than a tree trunk. The only way to get the trunk to flatten was to make hundreds of slits into it until it was so splintered that it would roll out like the cover of a roll top desk. This produced hard, rough, flat floors with lots of cracks in them, which saved us a lot of sweeping. Of course little kids could crawl under the house and get a view of our lives from the bottom up, but oh, well . . .

"So, how do you like your new home?" Dad proudly asked his bride. He didn't carry her across the threshhold. If he had, the Machiguengas would still be talking about this woman who couldn't even get onto the porch of her own house.

"It's beautiful," Mom answered breathlessly. The view *was* breathtaking, but remember she had also just survived her first climb up the bank from the river.

The Machis went out of their way to be helpful to us once they had recovered from the initial shock of seeing so much sickly white skin. The women kept us well supplied with bananas and fresh manioc. Victor, the headman of the community, made sure that the men regularly brought us fish and wild game. All day every day visitors came to sit on the porch and watch us, or to pick and eat lice out of each other's hair while they passed the time of day.

To survive, everyone but me had to learn the language. I could already get anything I needed by bawling and banging my head on the floor, something my Dad took care of later on.

"Here," he said, "you wanna bang your head on the floor? Let me help you." Nowadays I suppose he'd be arrested for using that approach, but it worked and he only had to do it once.

Terry started picking up Machiguenga along with English and some Spanish that Don Juan taught him. He frequently came home saying things Dad and Mom still couldn't understand. Fortunately.

For Dad and Mom, learning Machiguenga was one of the most exciting and brain busting things they would ever do. They worked at it from dawn to dark. During the day they didn't have much time for anything formal, but they could both entertain guests and get language data by leaping, sitting, standing, laughing, crying, spitting, and carrying on their weird lives on the front porch. They faithfully wrote down what people said when they did funny things, even if they weren't sure what it all meant. Like when Dad jumped up and down on the porch.

"*Tata gakeri?*" the Machiguenga's asked each other, wondering what had gotten ahold of him.

"Quick, Betty, write it down — '*Tata gakeri*' means 'he's jumping'." It didn't, but how were they to know? They sorted it out after making fools of themselves a few times.

Mostly during the day Mom and Dad had to carry water from the little stream beside our house, hunt for firewood, cook over a kerosene stove, boil drinking water, wash diapers and hand out medicine, sometimes pushing it down the throats of screaming, thrashing kids who would rather have died than swallow crystoids and epsom salts to kill their worms.

In the evenings after Terry and I had been tucked into our screened cribs and the Indians had gone home, they studied notebooks full of new words and analyzed the grammar by the light of a gasoline lantern. Ever so slowly words and phrases started to make sense.

Mom's brain is magnetic — heard just once, words stuck. Her first complete phrase, proudly practiced on Terry and me, was *"Gara piati anta."* She learned it by listening to a Machiguenga legend and now she could fluently say to us, "Don't go over there." "Don't go over there." "Don't go over there," all day long. If it hadn't been for Dad, we wouldn't ever have gotten to go anywhere. His first phrase was probably something like, "Sure, go wherever you like, but don't blame me if you get killed."

For many months the outwardly helpful Machiguengas were inwardly suspicious of our motives for being there. Families from upriver frequently visited us, but they kept their distance. The only outsiders they had known came to take advantage of them. Men with several wives were afraid that Dad, who was stuck with just one, would try to take their extras. Or at least take advantage of them. Women thought we'd steal their children for slaves.

Everyone figured it was only a matter of time until we made them work for us. That was one of the reasons why my folks did all their own chores in the early days. That and the fact that the Machiguengas didn't know how to wash clothes, cook on a stove or change diapers.

They may have been afraid of us, but it didn't take long for the word to get out that our house was full of magic and they were welcome to explore it to their hearts' content. Our kerosene refrigerator used a flame at the bottom to make ice at the top. In the mornings we talked into a box on the shelf and an invisible midget talked back. Our special needles and potions cured anything from hookworm to malaria.

Besides our great magic, two things helped break down their suspicions. The first was that we were a complete family with children just like theirs, and we obviously wanted to learn to talk to them in Machiguenga, even if it was taking an unbelievably long time to learn it. Their own babies learned it faster.

The Machis laughed at us endlessly, knowing we couldn't understand what they were saying. Eventually Dad and Mom got even. One day early on they left their tape recorder running on the front porch while their visitors laughed and joked. Months later they played the tape back for the same Machis, who realized that they'd been caught, so to speak, with their robes down.

The second ice breaker was that Dad and Mom tried to return the Machis' kindness in practical ways. Mom made dresses, including one from feed sacks for Victor's wife, and cooked fudge and popcorn for parties.

Dad became the local gunsmith, making firing pins from nails and cleaning corrosion off rusted shotguns. Machiguenga men thought he was the best thing since steel knives. He also became the village barber, cutting jagged crewcuts that made everyone look like Navy recruits.

It was a great place to be amateur seamstresses, barbers and entertainers. The Machis appreciated every little gesture, and wore their hacked hair and somewhat improvised new clothes with obvious pride.

Since more than half of the tribe's babies died as infants and life expectancy was less than forty years, medical magic also had a lot of appeal, at least after everything else had failed. Even though my folks' medical training was minimal, sometimes a shot in the dark was just the right treatment. For more difficult cases they could use the two-way radio to consult Dr. Eichenberger, SIL's resident physician at Yarinacocha. For very special cases, they called a plane to fly patients to Yarinacocha.

Of course, the medical efforts weren't always terribly successful. When Dad got back from his first trip in response to a request for urgent help, he wasn't very upbeat.

He'd taken off in a canoe with a couple of Indians and traveled three hours upriver. Along the way the canoe turned over and he was thrown into the flooded Urubamba with a notebook of language data. He and the notebook went in different directions.

Having gone as far as the canoe could go, Dad and his companions walked barefoot up a stream, crossing it fifteen times in water up to their waists. They found two people sick with malaria, but could only say that someone would have to come down for medicine as his was spoiled when the canoe turned over.

When Dad got home from that little excursion, Terry had a fever and I had a rash that looked something like measles. Mom told the headman about it, and most of the villagers fled in a panic, dreading the possibility of an epidemic. It turned out to not be measles, but we were left to our own devices for a while, since our radio had just quit working and we had no contact with Yarinacocha.

Many of our new friends died of simple diseases like the flu. Others, depressed because of inconsolable grief, hopeless marital problems or illegitimate pregnancies, committed suicide by drinking the juice of a poisonous root. In the village of Pangoa, just upriver from Timpia, eleven people killed themselves during our first year with the Machiguengas.

One man who lived up the Timpia from us brought his son down on a balsa raft soon after we got there. Dad and Mom examined him right where he sat on the raft and found an advanced case of tuberculosis, with open, running sores on the boy's neck. They couldn't even tell him that they couldn't help him — they had no medicine for tuberculosis.

The boy was obviously extremely sick, and his father didn't want his son to die close to where other people lived. Dad and Mom watched in frustrated, mute helplessness as the father pushed the raft off into the current with the boy still on it, hoping that he would be carried a long way down river before falling into the water to drown. After all, the farther away he died, the less likely it would be that his soul could make it back upriver to grab others to take with him.

Years later, as I write this story, tears run down my cheeks. I see that little boy sitting all alone on a tippy raft, trembling and wide eyed, trying to turn for a last look at the father who had just pushed him away. He was too sick even to cry. Although I don't even remember him, I cry for him now.

When our friend Rosa's little girl died in our house, we heard the heartbreaking wail of a woman in despair. We kept the body overnight.

In the morning, Rosa arrived back at our house wearing a red bandana. She had cut off all her hair so that her daughter's soul couldn't grab her and take her along to the place of the dead. Dad went with her to bury the little body. Machiguengas dread the dead so much that a woman usually has to bury her own husband or children without help.

Months washed past as rainy season approached. The rivers got higher and browner, the trails slicker, the nights cooler. Thunderous downpours streamed off our thatched roof. Sandbars and rocky beaches drowned. Everything we owned turned green. Chickens got crabby, ducks got slap happy.

In September I'd had my first birthday, complete with Don Juan, one candle and four balloons. Now, so soon, Christmas was coming. It was about time to wrap up our first six months in Timpia and go back to Yarinacocha for a while. Our clothes were wearing out. Food was running out. Energy was draining out. About all we had left in abundance was milk and oatmeal. In Yarinachocha we could regroup and Dad and Mom could work more intensely on their linguistic data.

One morning Dad started the generator that powered our repaired radio and called the operator at Yarinacocha. The news that came our direction wasn't what we anticipated.

"Wayne, we've got some problems with the Aeronca. Looks like we're going to have to send the engine to the U.S. for repairs. How copy? Over."

"Roger, Yarina. What's your best guess as to how long that will take? Over." The Aeronca was the only plane that could land near Timpia.

"Well, we're working on it as fast as we can, but it's going to take a while. Are you going to be okay out there? Over."

"We'll manage. We've got the essentials and the Machis are taking good care of us. Over."

"Our prayers are with you all. Say hi to Betty and the boys. Over and out."

We settled in for the duration, however long that might be. The first order of business was to figure how to celebrate Christmas without cards, mail, decorations or presents from the outside world. Kind of the way Mary and Joseph did it.

There were still some flour sacks left over from Victor's wife's dress, with a cute floral print on them. In addition, Mom had brought along some crochet thread. That was enough for starters.

Dad unleashed the sewing machine and started cranking. Mom got out her crochet needles, asked for cotton from her neighbors and went to work. By the time Christmas arrived, Terry and I each had a flowery flour sack suit from Dad and a freshly crocheted, cotton stuffed toy animal from Mom. I wish I could remember it — it sounds like what Christmas should be.

We even had a Christmas party in the Machiguenga's big communal house, which looked like a huge furry cocoon. It was a long oval with a dirt floor and stubby three-foot walls. With no windows, almost no light or fresh air could filter through. The only opening was a door on one side. In the mornings and evenings smoke from cook fires seeped through the thatch and the cracks in the walls, giving the whole house a bluish tinge.

Inside their house it was so dark that we could hardly move around without tripping over something. Cook fire smoke filled the house, leaving a shiny coating of black tar on everything. It was one big room with separate sleeping platforms for some of the occupants.

Hand carved wooden cooking utensils, bows and arrows, backstrap looms and other necessities were stuck in the vines that held the thatch on. Water gourds sat beside the cook fires, along with the thorny roots used to grate manioc. On the fires, boiling meat, bananas or manioc simmered in clay pots with banana leaf lids. Above the fires, blackened meat and leftovers smoked on vine racks suspended from the ceiling.

Victor, his two wives and all of their children lived together in that one house, along with a few other Indians. It was one big happy family, if you happened to be the favorite wife, and healthy. For the others, it could be pretty miserable.

With light from our gas lantern, the house was bright enough for the Christmas party, complete with a home made pinata, popcorn, candy and games. The Machiguengas weren't too sure about games like pin the tail on the Tapir, but the refreshments were a big hit. All in all it was a great time, except that they couldn't figure out why we were doing it. Dad and Mom didn't know yet how to tell them what Christmas was.

During our extended time, we learned to live and love in new ways. The Machiguengas were a fun people. They hid behind trees to jump out and scare us. They laughed at and with us. They carried Terry and me on fishing expeditions, and on outings to their gardens. They teased each other mercilessly, and considered anger one of the worst sins. We enjoyed being with them.

They were also a fearful people who couldn't enjoy a lot of the beauty around them. They didn't dare look at stunning sunsets or double rainbows for fear of getting diarrhea or being bitten by a snake. Army ants would march off with their children's souls, they feared. Eating deer would make them turn into one when they died. While we could sit on a mat and watch a lunar eclipse in a crystal clear sky, they erupted in total panic. After all, if the moon were to die, then the manioc the moon had supposedly given them would also disappear and they would starve to death.

The beautiful jungle that we loved and enjoyed was often dreadful to them, filled with spirits that were just waiting to make them sick or kill them. If an invisible being tricked them into having sexual intercourse with it, death was inevitable. They ran from things we never saw.

My parents, of course, had their own fears. Dad was never inclined to stay in one place for very long, so he made trips here and there during our stay in Timpia. When he left, Mom put our folding table across the doorless doorway to the bedroom and stood a shotgun by her mosquito net. Fortunately she was never threatened by wild animals or intruders. Given her total lack of experience with guns of any kind, she would undoubtedly have demolished all of our equipment, herself and both of her kids before she ever hit what was coming through the doorway.

In the end, it took three months to get the Aeronca engine fixed and installed. The milk and oatmeal never ran out, and the Indians kept us supplied with food, including enough green squash to make anyone grow up hating it, which I did.

By the time we got back to Yarinacocha we had been with the Machiguengas for nine months straight, and white people looked as strange to us as we had to the

Machis. Just returning to our little center was a total shock. We got off the plane late in the afternoon and walked directly to the group dining room for supper with our friends. Uncle Cam asked us to stand up as he welcomed us back to Yarina. Then he got a twinkle in his eye.

"Now you see why I don't want teams to be out in the village for more than six months at a time," he laughed.

Apparently we looked, and smelled, and acted like Machiguengas. Which is just what we wanted.

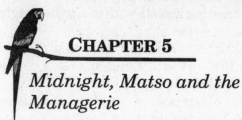

CHAPTER 5

Midnight, Matso and the Managerie

Although the Machiguengas gave us lots of chances to practice, we didn't have much luck with pets. Or I suppose you could say our pets didn't have much luck with us, since we always survived and they often didn't.

Our sociable river otter, with the sleek

brown skin and liquid body, gave us no end of laughs swimming and fishing with us in the lake before he drowned all alone in his own little swimming pool.

Then we had a squirrel monkey, which nobody liked and he liked us even less. He'd bitten people on the lip and several other places before dying of heat stroke on our front porch. It was his own fault — no one dared get close enough to move him into the shade. No one shed a tear.

My own squirrel monkey, Reepacheep, who was about as loving and fun a pet as any boy could have, ended up hanging himself in his own cage after spending hours hunting insects with me in the jungle. I did shed a tear.

Tiahuaca, our funny little dog that we left in the care of the Indians for a couple months, died of a snake bite.

Some of our pets didn't die as soon as we wished they would. Our boas got tangled around the plumbing behind our toilet in Yarina and had to be forcibly removed. Our giant toucan perched in a mango tree right above the trail to our back door and whanged unsuspecting passers by on the top of the head with his long sharp beak. The trumpet birds that perched on the peak of our thatched roof trumpeted and hummed along as we sang choruses during evening devotions, then brazenly pecked our legs during the daytime, completely forgetting anything they had learned during the Bible reading.

Even with our bad luck we persisted in always having an exotic animal or two around the house, since the Machiguengas were always bringing home live animals they had caught. Usually they were babies left behind when their mothers were killed by hunters.

Nowadays I'd think twice about keeping wild animals as pets, but growing up in the jungle it was about as natural as having a dog or a cat, except that most of us don't end up eating our dogs and cats.

Machiguengas didn't know about endangered species, so they just ate whatever they could kill and tamed whatever they could catch live. Their version of living in harmony with the jungle involved cutting it down to make gardens and hunting any animals or birds within a day's walk or canoe ride. That included beautiful macaws, exotic monkeys and wild tapirs. They were all, I must say, delicious.

Machiguengas sometimes went to great

pains to keep their unusual pets alive. Often in the early mornings or late afternoons we could sit by a cook fire and watch women feed their birds. They'd chew up cassava or bananas, squoosh a gooey ball of it to the front of their mouths and let the birds gobble it from right between their lips. Or they'd sit and breast feed monkeys, cuddling them in their laps like furry babies.

Still and all, the Indians never lost track of the difference between animals and people, and their pets often ended up in the pot. Hunting dogs got a special lack of consideration — they had to be kept semi-starved so they'd hunt better. Most village dogs were racks of sores and bones, frequently beaten with sticks and almost always tied to a house post with a short vine.

Anyway, Midnight was our black spider monkey. He was all black with a small head and pointed tufts of hair that stuck out like bushy sideburns in front of his little ears. He had a small body, but his arms, legs and tail were long and dangly like black octopus arms attached to a ball of black fur. His big black eyes, raised eyebrows and crew cut hair always made him look like a surprised little old man.

The best part of Midnight was his tail. It was about two and a half feet long and bare underneath. He used it even more than his arms and legs. In his cage, or in the trees, or in our arms, that tail would slither out like a boa constrictor and wrap around a branch or a swing or our necks. Since he loved to be carried around, and hated his cage, trying to get him off us could take two people. One unwrapped his tail and the other held the rest of him while he barked and squirmed and grabbed at things with his long skinny fingers and toes.

In the jungle, spider monkeys are a wild bunch. Every once in a while we'd see a group of ten or twenty of them eating ripe fruit and new leaves fifty or sixty feet above us while we were out hunting. Since they usually felt pretty safe, they often didn't take off right away. First they threatened us by barking, growling and breaking off dead branches to drop on us.

Then, at the first blast of a shotgun or rifle, or the first hit with an arrow, the whole group raced off through the tree tops with trapeeze leaps and swings. Branches shook and broke and the jungle was filled with noise.

Down below, we ran to keep up, charging pell mell through the trees and undergrowth. When you're running through the jungle, it's not a bad idea to watch where you're going so you don't run into stickers, trip over vines and fall into burrows. Unfortunately, when you're following monkeys you always have to be looking up, and monkey sprints usually ended with us looking as if we'd been raked, shredded and beaten. Sometimes it was more fun than we could stand.

Unless the monkeys paused out of curiosity or just to catch their breath, it was hopeless. Even the Machiguengas had a hard time shooting a gun or aiming an arrow at flying monkeys while ducking under bushes, wiping huge cobwebs off their faces, hesitating to yank thorns out of their bare feet and slaloming around trees at full speed. If Terry and I were along, they always had to come back and find us wherever we'd gotten lost along the way.

Female monkeys carrying babies had a bit of a disadvantage, so it wasn't unusual to kill a mother with a tiny baby clinging tightly to her fur. If the baby survived the fall, it was taken home to be raised as a pet, and that's how we got Midnight.

Midnight, Matso and the Managerie

We took Midnight from the village to Yarinacocha at the end of the summer when we went back in for school. He spent his days in a big cage eating bananas and papayas or going for walks with us, wrapping his long arms and legs and tail clear around us. Any time we let him loose he caused too much trouble, like swinging from the curtains in our house or eating the neighbor's fruit, so he rarely got any freedom.

After just a few months with us, Midnight came to a humiliating end. One night he escaped from his cage and went in search of a midnight snack, so to speak. About a hundred yards from our house was the center's fruit shed, where fruit was warehoused for the group cafeteria and for sale. Dozens of stalks of bananas hung from the rafters and bins of papayas lined the walls. Midnight thought he'd died and gone to heaven when he broke in.

In the morning, Midnight wasn't feeling well. Nor was the person who managed the fruit shed, but at least he didn't have a severe case of diarrhea. Throughout the day Midnight drained his feast through the bottom of the cage, and by late afternoon dehydration had done him in.

With a quiet little ceremoney we buried Midnight in our back yard under a cross with his name on it. We grieved the loss of our monkey, but marked the spot so we could dig him up later and see what his bones looked like. When we did, he hadn't quite finished turning back into dust, and the slimy, smelly mess we found kept us out of his grave forever.

Matso was a whole different story. From the moment I first laid eyes on him, sitting in his seller's lap at the airport, I knew I had to have him. After all, how often do you get the chance to own an ocelot cub?

I don't even remember how much I paid for him, but it was probably in the exorbitant range of $20.00, including his rope leash. Once at our house, of course, he had the run of the place. Unfortunately that meant a lot of noise at night, since he didn't sleep when we did. The good part of it was that we didn't have trouble with rats while he lived with us.

'Matso' was short for '*matsontsori*', or 'ocelot' in Machiguenga. He had huge golden brown eyes and a matching coat of stiff hair with tawny yellow and black spots in it. His tongue, even at that young age, would put a wood rasp to shame.

I had never seen a wild ocelot alive in the jungle. They usually hunt at night and spend many hours walking, often on man-made trails. During the day they stay well hidden in thick brush or under fallen trees. Their most common contact with the Machiguengas was to eat their chickens, something Matso knew about even without his parents around to teach him. Machiguengas shot ocelots on sight, both to preserve their flocks and to sell the skins, which were worth a small fortune.

When I first got Matso, his coat looked as if it were worth about two cents. Presumably his mother would have kept him in better condition, but she wasn't around and I wasn't about to lick him 'til he shone. So I decided to bathe him.

There isn't much to compare with the difficulty of bathing a wild cat. Mom agreed to help me, a decision she would regret forever. Matso was small and inexperienced, but he knew exactly how he felt about bath water and knew just how to express his feelings with his teeth and claws.

By the time we were done with the shampoo and towel, most of Matso's orange color had washed out and most of our blood had drained out. Whatever we accomplished wasn't worth it, and we never did it again.

Often in the mornings Matso woke me up by licking my ears with his rough tongue. I found his bright eyes and playful spirit irresistable, but my ears were nearly ground off in the process.

Of course we had to feed him raw meat. The hope, foolish as it seems now, was to get him so used to the meat we fed him that he would have no inclination to hunt. That hope was dashed the first night he escaped and went cruising.

Sad to say, our neighborhood was full of exotic meals. We weren't the only family at Yarina with fabulous pets. Just down from us, for example, the Shanks family had a stunning blue and gold macaw that had been in the family for twenty five years.

Shanks' macaw knew all the kids' names and voices, and could cry, laugh and yell like the best of them. To its everlasting credit, it never learned to imitate Martha's violin practice, but it pretty much got the rest of the family routines down pat. In fact, it could carry on family arguments all by itself, sitting in their mango tree and reciting all the parts.

Squawky the macaw had a special place

to sit in front of the house. Sometimes he was kept there by a little chain, and that's how Matso found him while out for his night on the town. In the morning Squawky had lost his squawk and was basically a pile of blue and gold feathers attached to a chain. Matso and my family were in a heap of big time trouble. In fact, Matso was headed for the chopping block when Uncle Jim, who loved all kinds of animals, saved him.

Uncle Jim thought he'd be able to reform Matso. That lasted until Matso discovered and then dismembered the flock of chickens in the back yard of the children's home. Although we all thought it fabulous that he hadn't forgotten how to hunt, his tastes were getting rather expensive. Survival of the fittest sounds like a great principle until the losers are all your neighbors' pets.

In the end, Matso went to a nearby zoo. It was him or us, and there wasn't room for the six of us in the cage they were going to give him.

Then there was Sahino, our little white-lipped peccary. When we got him he was a cute bundle of bristles and about as fun to cuddle as a wire brush. He was the orphaned survivor of a pig hunt and already incredibly agile.

Domesticated piglets are pretty helpless for a long time. Baby peccaries, on the other hand, take off after their mothers within a few hours of being born. In the jungle there isn't much time for lounging around while you're learning to walk.

Our first attempts at a pig pen were laughable. He jumped out of boxes, fences, cages. Fortunately, having him out wasn't actually that big a problem, since he had pretty well bonded to our family and would never run off. I don't know if it was our smell or our food that made him feel so at home. Whatever, he stuck around the house. Explored around the house. Rooted around the house. Found our stash of special treats.

Now remember, when we went out to live with the Machiguengas for several months at a time, we had to take all of our precious supplies with us in small planes like Aeroncas, Helios and Cessnas. Our weight allowance was so restrictive that often we poured out extra drinking water before squeezing into the plane. Everything on board was absolutely essential to our survival, we thought, including the can of real butter that would provide special treats over the next several months. On our birthdays, for example, we'd get butter with our crackers and think we were just the luckiest kids in the whole wide world.

Our pig didn't know about rationing, and we didn't know the pig liked butter. When he started, *he* probably didn't even know he liked butter. Still, there it was, hidden under Dad and Mom's bed with the rest of our goodies, in a can that just had a flimsy tin foil wrapper on it. And no one was looking.

By the time someone went into the bedroom, there were butter smears all over the pona floor, little shreds of buttered tin foil scattered everywhere, and a butterfat, butter-faced pig sticking his tongue out as far as he could to lick the butter off his eyebrows. We licked his prickly hide, yelled at him in Machiguenga and nearly made him throw it all up.

When we all flew back to Yarinacocha, a few days later, we took Sahino with us. There was no place to stash him, so he rode on Mom's lap for a couple hours, having buttered her up in the days since his gluttonous forage.

Back at Yarina, Sahino went up to the center's experimental farm to live with his more civilized cousins. Dad hoped to breed him with domesticated pigs and produce a hardy, healthy super pig that would weigh 400 pounds and leap tall buildings in a single jump. First we had to contain him long enough for him to fall in love with a fat sow.

Apparently he wasn't enchanted, and he managed to jump out of everything we put him in. Finally, in desperation, we emptied a fifty-five gallon barrel that we used to store our belongings when we were going to be away for a while. The barrel was about 26 inches in diameter and forty inches high. There was no room for Sahino to move, much less get a running start. By morning, he had jumped straight out.

Unfortunately, we had to give up before we could introduce high-fly bacon to the world. With no way to contain him, we ended up doing what any good Machiguenga would have done. We ate him. He had that rich buttery flavor that you don't often get in the jungle.

CHAPTER 6

Arturo & Maria

When 16-year-old Arturo started
stealing boiled manioc and fish from

14-year-old Maria's little clay cook pot, we knew they were madly in love. It was one of the sweetest Machiguenga romances we would ever see. And one of the saddest. Romeo and Juliet in the village of Etariato.

Our own lives had gotten sort of nomadic, going back and forth between the Timpia and Yarinacocha in six-month cycles. At Yarinacocha we had a lot of support services like the school, print shop, consultants, clinic, radio shop, hangar and so on. It was a good place for Dad and Mom to make progress on language analysis and linguistic writeups, away from the pressures of tribal life.

In the tribal area there were several scattered families that we visited, but Dad and Mom kind of thought Timpia would be our primary home for a while. Nothing is ever so simple — when we got ready to go back to Timpia for our third long stay, almost all of the Machiguengas had left because of the school.

SIL and the Peruvian government had recently agreed to work together on starting bilingual schools all over the jungle. SIL's part was to help identify potential teachers, give them some training in teaching the three Rs, and develop school books.

Of course a lot of the first recruits could barely read, and even more couldn't speak the Spanish they were supposed to teach. Many hadn't ever seen a school. It took a pretty good imagination to think of them as the hope of the jungle, educationally.

When Dad first proposed the idea of a school to the Machiguengas at Timpia, Moran went with him to do the talking. Moran was a Machiguenga who had had a little schooling downriver with the Piro Indians. Mostly Moran did the talking because Dad's Machiguenga was still no match for the Indians' traditional oratorical style.

As usual, Moran spoke only to Victor, the head man at Timpia. Not that you would have known he was talking to Victor — it would have been rude to look at the person he was talking to so he looked away or just kept his head down. Out of cultural courtesy, Victor repeated back to him everything he said, phrase by phrase. Others who sat in the communal house listening to every word would never have admitted to knowing anything that was going on until Victor talked to each of them individually. If Dad happened to hear any of the conversation, it was purely accidental, as far as they were concerned.

Moran explained what the government wanted to do, talked about what a school was, described some of the logistics and listed the things the Machiguengas would be responsible for. The rise and fall of the staccato-like dialogue went on for three hours. Finally, they ran out of steam.

"Well, what did they say?" Dad was pretty much in the dark.

"They say they're going hunting tomorrow."

"So what does that mean?"

"It means they'll talk about it and let us know later."

The Machiguengas did agree to a school, and to Abelino as the first teacher. We were at Yarinacocha when they actually got started, and since there was no school house yet, the students sat or lay on the floor of our empty house while they did their lessons.

Peruvian government regulations required that all children six and up be in school. The problem was that the Machiguengas didn't know how old anyone was. They didn't even have a way of counting past four. Moran had to just make rough estimates.

"Reach over your head and touch your ear." If a kid could do it, he must be at least six.

"Have you lost all four of your front teeth?" the teacher would ask while examining the student's mouth, horselike. If so, and four new teeth had come in, they'd be at least eight. Every new student got a birthdate on the spot, not that they could ever remember what it was, or cared.

To make matters worse, none of the students had names, since they lived in family groupings and kinship terms had always been all they needed. Abelino had to make up names, and then try to talk the students into sticking with the same names year after year. It didn't always work.

Most of the twenty-one children and adults started out having never held a pencil before. They looked at their books upside down, sideways and occasionally even right side up.

The Machiguengas were excited about their school and eager to learn. Don Juan, on the other hand, was fiercely opposed to it.

"Teaching the Indians to read, write and count will do them no good, and it will upset the nature of things," he argued. "They have their place here, we have our place here, and changing all of that will ruin everything."

In particular, "ruining everything" included losing the opportunity to exploit the Machiguengas' ignorance. Don Juan was a good and intelligent man, but his opinions came from quite a different world from my parents'. To get a little support for his position, he invited the priests from downriver to set up a mission at Timpia.

The Indians who lived in and around Timpia were primitive, but not dumb. They figured out right off that living with a patron, a priest and an SIL linguistic team all in the same small clearing wasn't going to be much fun. They had already had their wives abused and children stolen by outsiders, so they decided to move out before the priest moved in.

Etariato, "Armour Fish Creek," was an hour and a half upriver, and seemed as good a spot as any to build a new village. There was nothing there but a sandy beach and dense jungle.

When we first arrived in Etariato in May, 1954, seven little "tambos" had been built on the beach. You can sort of think of tambos as Machiguenga tents, except that they weren't portable. The Indians could whip one together in a couple of hours by lashing together some cane poles and covering the frame with cane leaves. The drier the leaves got, the more they leaked, but you could always throw more leaves on top until the whole thing collapsed. By then, hopefully, you were gone. Biodegradable tents. We loved sleeping in them, except that the leaves had sawtooth edges so you had to be careful about rubbing against them.

Our very own tambo was about 9 x 12 feet with a seven-foot peak, which sounds pretty spacious for a tent but not so spacious when it had to include a kitchen, dining room, bedroom, office, living room and clinic.

Besides, there were six of us now. My sister Sandy had been born five months earlier in the tiny clinic at Yarinacocha between stays in Timpia. Anita also lived with us. She was a Machiguenga girl who helped with babysitting and housekeeping and language study when she wasn't in school herself.

"How are we all going to fit in here?" Mom wondered out loud. For one thing, even though the roof was high enough for them, they couldn't get past one another when the table was inside.

"Well, I'll build a platform on the back of the tambo for the boys' jungle hammock," Dad suggested. We'll just set it on the platform and they'll at least have a roof and mosquito net. Then if we move our table outside at night Anita will have a place to sleep inside. At least it's not raining yet, so we can just keep a bunch of our stuff outside too. I don't think it'll take them long to get us a real house built."

The jungle hammock idea conveniently ignored the fact that someone had seen a jaguar swimming across the river toward the village one afternoon. Not that the inside of the open tambo would have been much safer than the jungle hammock's flimsy netting.

Our tambo looked like a gypsy camp. A 55 gallon barrel of gasoline stood in front, with an assortment of bottles and cans on it. Wash basins hung from the roof. Boxes and five-gallon cans of supplies were stacked here and there. Towels and dirty clothes were draped over the half wall at the front. Pots and pans littered the yard.

The school kept right on going in a tambo of its own. Students wrote and doodled in the sand under their feet, and ran to the river for recess. Most of the kids were dressed in rags — remnants of old cushmas. They studied all morning and then went to help clear land and build houses in the afternoon.

It was great to be living just like the Indians, with damp dirty sand always stuck to us and a river right outside our front door. Sandy was always sandy, even though she spent a lot of time in a crib so she wouldn't eat the stuff. Terry and I cooked fish over stick fires in our own little cook pots and invited our Machi friends to join us for meals. One day we even got into a canoe and pushed off so we could pretend to pole it. In a split second Dad had yelled for help and stripped to his boxers, but before he could come after us a Machiguenga had chased us down. The Urubamba was fast and cold and no place for a three and four year old, I guess.

Behind us machetes rang and axes whacked all day as the Machiguengas cleared land for houses and gardens, on the hill behind us.

After a few weeks on the beach, we flew up to Pangoa, a village above the Pongo, where another school was just starting. We hoped that our new house at Etariato would be built while we were gone.

Pangoa's headman, Señor Pereira, had a Machiguenga mother and a Brazilian father. He was a brilliant man who had earned a gold medal at the University of Cuzco but didn't get it because he was half Indian. Rumor has it he then got involved in an argument over a woman and killed his rival, after which he fled to Machiguenga land, never to leave again.

Señor Pereira was a man without a people. To outsiders he was an Indian; to the Indians he was a white man. For sixty years he lived with multiple wives and dozens of his own children overseeing a work force of up to 400 Machiguenga men who helped him cultivate coffee, rubber trees and cacao beans that were used to make chocolate.

Although he never left the area again, he was a walking encyclopedia of local and world events. He knew more about Chinese inventions and discoveries than the Chinese did. Whenever we went to visit him, we took newspapers and magazines that he memorized as he read them.

It was Señor Pereira who wanted to get a school started, and who chose his daughter Antonina to be the teacher. Most of his own children were bilingual from listening to their father's long discussions at the dinner table, and many had gone upriver to Catholic schools. Several became teachers, leaders and special friends of ours. Two of his daughters had been my first baby sitters.

All in all they were a brilliant family, and Señor Pereira was glad to have my parents there to help with the school. Not that he wanted Dad and Mom to meddle in anything else — he didn't get along with anyone who interfered on his turf.

The first part of August Dad, Terry and I flew back to Etariato so Dad could push the new house along. Mom and Sandy would wait a couple of weeks and then fly down to join us.

The house was a long way from being done. It didn't have a roof or walls and only had a small bit of floor so far. One of the headmen was upset because some of his family wanted to believe in my parents' God, so he had halted construction. When Mom and Sandy arrived we were still in the tambo and stayed there until the gnats drove us crazy. Then, ready or not, we moved into our house frame on the high hill and hoped it wouldn't start raining for a couple of more months.

The morning after we moved in the black sky fell on us. It rained buckets. Gushed torrents. Water soaked our heaped supplies. Terry and I ate breakfast in our rain capes, with the hoods shielding our faces. Rainwater filled our cereal bowls as fast as we could empty them, diluting the milk and chilling the oatmeal. Sandy had a little tarp over her crib, but as soon as we all finished eating we rushed to the school to sit by a fire in the back corner and warm up while the students did their lessons.

It rained for two days. The river rose and turned an angry, churning brown. Upriver, three Machiguengas rode the crest on a five-log raft loaded with most of our equipment and supplies for the next three months. Mom had left the stuff behind because it wouldn't fit into the plane, and asked the Indians to just store it in one of their houses until the next plane stopped there. Instead, the Machiguengas decided to do us the favor of bringing it down by raft.

A few moments of tenseness, and then the raft rushed into the Pongo and crashed into a canyon wall. Sixteen boxes of food supplies, a carton of soap, two five-gallon cans of baby food, a duffle bag full of cooking pots and utensils, the sewing machine and Mom's precious accordian flew into the water. Two of the Machiguengas hung on. The third was thrown off and barely managed to catch back up to the raft. They arrived embarrassed and nearly empty handed, having salvaged little of the cargo. We thanked God that they had arrived.

About the time everything we still had was dried and reorganized, another rainstorm hit and we went through it all again. The Indians were moving ahead with our roof, but they had to haul the leaves from some distance.

Family arguments, sickness and even death slowed things down, as well as long drinking parties that left the men incapacitated for days at a time. They drank a special brew that their wives made by chewing up manioc and spitting it into a huge wooden tub. By the time that stuff had fermented for a while, it was pretty potent. One of my greatest accomplishments in life was taking a drink of it once and keeping it down. Anyway, with all those delays it took three months to get a roof over our heads.

September 15 was my third birthday. For a birthday present, Mario and his friends made me my first real set of bow and arrows so I wouldn't have to play with toy ones anymore. I couldn't believe my good fortune. Since Terry got a set too, we could hunt each other.

Grandma and Grandpa Elkins, who I only knew through letters and packages, had sent us a couple of angel food cake and ice cream mixes. The ice cream was easy, since we had a kerosene refrigerator with a tiny freezer. The cake was a bit harder. For an hour and a half Dad and Mom took turns beating it with a fork, trying to get the egg whites to stand up. By the time my party started, they were exhausted. The cake and ice cream were fabulous.

That night after it was all over, I made a decision that would change my life forever.

Every night we had Bible reading and family prayers by the light of our gas lantern. Usually we sang choruses together, even though Dad couldn't carry a tune to save his soul and Terry and I weren't much better. In fact, the best part of our singing was Mom and our two pet trumpet birds that roosted on the roof. Something about our music always fired them up and they joined right in.

Dad always passed around prayer

Arturo & Maria

requests for each of us.

"Ronny, how about if you pray for the Townsends. Terry, would you pray for Grandma and Grandpa?" And so on.

This time, I just ignored my request and poured out my heart to God, asking Jesus to come into my heart and take away all of my badness. I didn't like it, I told him. I may have been only three, but God listened, and I've never doubted that He took me seriously.

"Where did God take your sins?" Dad and Mom asked me afterwards.

"He threw them over the bank behind our house," I answered. That was where we and the Indians threw all of our garbage.

I wasn't the only one thinking seriously about spiritual things. The Machiguengas often asked questions about God, about creation, about the spirits, and about what would happen to them when they died. Some wanted to make Jesus their headman. Some adamantly opposed him, including Felix.

"Just let that person they call Jesus come around to bother me. I'll show him who's headman here. I'll fight him and send him on his way," he announced one day.

Arturo and Maria were some of the first

to decide they wanted to follow Jesus, and that's what made their courtship so special.

Arturo was one of the students in the school. He had run away from his master downriver so that he could live near us at Etariato and go to school. He was bright, fun, a good teacher and a natural leader.

Maria moved in with us right after our house was built, along with a few other kids whose parents lived too far from the school. By then we had a kitchen at one end of the house, an open breezeway in the middle and one big bedroom on the other end.

Beyond the bedroom was an enclosed section with a dirt floor and a four foot wall around it. That's where Maria and the other kids stayed, sleeping on a mat on the ground and cooking their meals in a little clay pot on a log fire. Terry and Sandy and I loved to sit around the fire with them and eat whatever they were cooking.

To show how much he liked her, Arturo snuck up to Maria's wall with an arrow, reached over and speared manioc and meat out of her pot. Hearts beat faster and romantic gossip spread like flu.

Even better, Arturo was catching fish and other meat for Maria and leaving it in the jungle where she could find it. After she'd cooked it, he'd steal it back. Wheweeee! That was about as romantic as it ever got in Etariato.

From watching them together, of course, you'd never guess they were madly in love. They never, never paid any attention to each other. That would have been pure scandal.

Throughout Maria's romantic courtship, she puzzled us with her pouting. One day she ran off into the jungle, and Mom went after her.

"Little brother, little brother, come home," Mom called. We used the same kinship terms they did instead of names, and if you really loved your little sister you called her "little brother."

Maria stayed in the jungle until after we'd gone to bed, then snuck back home. Later Mom wanted to talk to her about it.

"Little brother, why is your face so sad?" Maria said nothing. Her secret was too painful to share.

In the meantime, Arturo built a small house for himself and Maria. When it was finished he came over to our house, took Maria by the hand and they eloped to his house.

There wasn't all that much difference

between eloping and a wedding, of course, but to be proper Arturo should have asked the headman for permission. If Victor had agreed to it, he would have personally put their hands together. Victor wasn't happy, so Arturo tried to placate him.

"I asked Don Walter for permission, and he said it was fine," Arturo claimed.

Dad figures that was the only Machiguenga couple he ever married, and he didn't even know he did it.

Just two weeks later, Maria suddenly got sick in school. Within a day she was dying. It was dark when Arturo frantically came to get Mom, but Mom had no idea what was wrong. Finally, as Maria lay twisting and turning on the ground, she looked up into Mom's face. Her final words were,

"Is it true? Will I go up high where God is?" She never heard the answer.

Too late, Maria's sister told us her secret. She was carrying a baby, but not Arturo's, and she was determined not to let him know. Pinching her stomach hadn't gotten rid of it, so she finally went into the jungle and drank a potion made from poisonous plants. She only wanted to abort the baby, but she drank too much. Within just two weeks, the most loving marriage we ever saw was over. Arturo never really recovered.

Dad and Mom helped Arturo bury Maria in a deep grave in a sand bar downriver. If the grave were dug too shallow, the Machiguengas thought, she might turn into a buzzard and come back to eat her own body. The few people who were beginning to understand a little about God sang a brand new Machiguenga song together beside the freshly turned dirt. "It is very beautiful up high. There is a house that Jesus is making for me."

That night Maria's neighbors heard her come back. "Ting, ting, ting." They told us about it the next morning.

"She came back looking for things she threw away while she was alive. She needs to take them with her. She even ran into the corner of the hut where the school children sleep and knocked it down." Sure enough, it had fallen during the night.

Then, five days later Anita came running to get Mom.

"Come and see what Andres has stuck with his arrow." Mom got her flashlight and followed Anita to where Andres was beating a furry animal. Anita was outraged.

"Can you believe that when Maria died

she didn't even have the decency to go live somewhere else. She turned into a possum and came right up the trail to where she used to live with Arturo and ate out of her old cooking pot."

Everyone struggled to sort out the differences between what they were seeing with their own eyes, and hearing from my parents about God's power over the spirits.

A few weeks after Maria died Melchor, a headman from up the Timpia, and his very pregnant wife came to visit us. They'd stayed with us a while back while my parents treated their son Victorino for tuberculosis. It was a long ordeal, but Victorino fully recovered, and Melchor was grateful.

Now they lay on the floor of our hut long after I fell asleep, listening to records and talking to my folks about God. It was hard to figure out the truth — did God really love them and offer them hope as Dad and Mom said, or had he abandoned them shortly after creation, as they had always believed?

Shortly after Melchor took his family back home, his wife died giving birth. Since there was no one to take care of the baby, they threw it into the grave too, stomping on the ground until it stopped crying. Then

Melchor got in his canoe to come back and see us.

"Tell me again about going up high. I don't want to go where the buzzards live."

"Oh, no," Dad explained, "I'm not talking about a place where buzzards live. I'm talking about a beautiful home that God is making for those who trust him and make Jesus their headman."

While he was there, Melchor prayed to God.

Even as a little boy I watched a lot of people die, sometimes by the dozens when flu epidemics hit the area. I also heard new babies come crying into the world while their mothers moaned. With open walls, we didn't miss out on much.

Mom's first proud delivery was Dorotea's baby. We heard someone come in the night to get Mom.

"Do you want me to help?" Dad asked.

"No, it's probably something a woman should do," Mom answered. Besides, she still had her textbook on obstetrics from Bible school days. Of course she'd never actually witnessed a birth, even though she'd had three babies herself.

When she got to Dorotea's house, Dorotea was laying on her back on her little sleeping platform and Mom could at least see what was going on. Unfortunately, what she saw coming out was a white balloon-like thing instead of the hairy black head she expected. She frantically grabbed her book and started flipping through pages to find out what it was and what she should do about it, but while she was flipping pages Dorotea climbed off the platform to squat on the dirt floor, where Mom couldn't see anything.

"Grab the baby," Dorotea frantically commanded, and Mom reached down to grab it but couldn't tell what she was grabbing and slippery little Pepe dropped in the dirt. Dorotea was horrified. Mom yelled for Dad to come and he got there in time to help wash Pepe and cut the cord with a pair of boiled scissors.

Pepe was never quite right, and maybe this explains it. On the other hand, maybe it's because he grew up with Terry and me as role models. We were friends for many years.

That same night while Dad and Mom were gone rats ate a hole in Dad's air mattress. It was never quite right after that either. Some nights, nothing goes right.

CHAPTER 7

Canoeing the Tushmo

I would never have voluntarily gone swimming in the Tushmo. It was a creepy inlet off Lake Yarinacocha that wound its way beside and then behind our linguistics center. The bottom was so gooshy that it sent prickles up and down my spine to think of ever putting my feet in it. There might be slithery creatures just waiting to chomp on bare toes.

Trees hung out over the narrow Tushmo. They were certainly picturesque, full of orioles and kingfishers and buzzards, but it wasn't hard to imagine snakes and iguanas and spiders dropping on your head when you drifted under them.

Certain seasons of the year the edges of the Tushmo were pea green with algae. It was so thick that anything that fell in came out looking Martian. Then when lily pad season came, the Tushmo filled wall to wall with lily pads, as if it had all been carpeted. You could hardly get a canoe through it. Of course when the lily pad season ended, they all died and rotted and a putrid stench filled the inlet.

Still, sometimes the Tushmo was a great place to canoe and fish, even if not to swim. In fact, the only time I can ever remember purposely swimming in it was at night when we were hunting alligators. In the darkness you couldn't see all the yucky stuff, so it wasn't nearly so scary. But that's another story.

One Saturday morning Mom thought it'd be fun to go on a family outing in the aluminum canoe. We'd been on furlough for a year, and it was such a relief to be back in the jungle.

For us kids, furloughs were a kind of necessary evil, with a few really nice benefits. We did a lot of traveling while our parents visited family, friends and supporters all over the United States. In exchange for pretending we were excited to visit people we didn't know, including our relatives, we got to see lots of the famous things between the Liberty Bell and the California redwoods.

It wasn't that our parents' friends and family weren't nice to us. Many of them went out of their way to help us feel welcome and entertained. It just wasn't very easy for them to figure out what to do with three little Indians.

Dad and Mom talked about their work in Peru and we climbed their friends' trees. We learned about Dairy Queen and A&W Root Beer stands in between slide shows at churches. Terry got hit by a truck while he and I were off shopping for ice cream sticks. Melody was born in Indiana, where Mom's parents lived. I started school, and that's about all I remember. We were homesick the whole time.

The fact that Terry and I were both school age when we got back to Peru was going to change our lives. Instead of getting to be in the tribe whenever our parents were, we would only get to be there during vacations from school. The rest of the time they were away from Yarinacocha, which was usually only between September and December, we would stay in the children's home, about a five-minute walk away from our own house.

There were many kids who lived at Yarinacocha full time. Their parents helped staff the school, fly and maintain the airplanes, repair radios, print school books for the Indians, administer the work and so on.

For the rest of us, the children's home wasn't such a bad place to be, even if we did prefer the tribe. It was kind of like living with a bunch of cousins, since the same kids ended up there for a few months each year. We had a lot of fun together. In fact, sometimes kids whose parents lived at Yarinacocha full time wished their parents would leave for a while so they could live in the children's home.

A lot of neat things happen when you get a dozen missionary kids together in one house for three months. I think maybe we enjoyed some of those things more than the house parents did. Like the rug rides we gave each other on the slick waxed mahogany floor in the huge living room. I especially remember one night when we had a bit of a catastrophe with the rug. It was several years later, after Sandy had started staying in the children's home with us.

Sandy was sitting on the rug holding one end of a rope. She was tough as nails and would never admit she was afraid, so she was a pretty good rug rider.

"I'm going to see how fast I can get you going. Don't you dare let go of the rope!" I knew she wouldn't, even if her life depended on it.

I grabbed the other end of the rope and kind of trotted her around the room to get her going. The tip of her tongue stuck out as she concentrated on holding on. Once she started gaining speed I could move closer to the middle of the room and just swing her around me like a sling.

For a few fabulous seconds she went so fast the rug nearly came off the floor like a flying carpet. Her hair blew in the wind and her mouth couldn't decide whether to smile or shriek. Then, for some reason her hands slipped and off she flew like a rock out of the sling. On her way to crashing into a wall she took out a dining room table leg, two little kids and a couple of chairs. I guess that's what the children's home parents didn't like about it, even though Sandy got right up with a big grin on her face.

Another great game for that many kids was "swat." We turned off all the lights in the house and used magazines to whack anyone we got close enough to. One night our temporary mother walked into the living room in the middle of a game and got pretty beat up before we realized who she was. It was her fault for not having her own magazine.

Anyway, my folks were pretty good about trying to find fun things to do together as a family when we could, to make up for times when we were apart. The outing in the aluminum canoe was probably meant to be one of those, but I'm not sure it was such a great idea, at least in hindsight.

At the time, we thought it would be a lot of fun. Melody was too young to go and Dad stayed home with her, but the rest of us all piled in. Since there were only four of us, we invited our friend Tim Townsend, or "Towner," to come along as well.

Mind you, we weren't crazy about the

aluminum canoe. It was slippery, noisy and
tippy, but it was all we could find to borrow
on short notice and it could carry a pretty
good load, which it was doing on this trip.
We headed straight for the Tushmo.

For half an hour or so we paddled up the
Tushmo, chattering and dipping our hands
in the water to tempt the piranhas. The
inlet narrowed as we went, until we could
almost reach out and touch branches on
both sides of us. Fish jumped, birds sang,
and the canoe leaked. The aluminum canoe
always leaked. We more or less glided along
in a zig zag line because that canoe was
hard to keep going straight.

It wasn't exactly a quiet, peaceful trip.
Every time we ran into a submerged log or
branch, which was pretty often, we could
hear it scraping the aluminum all the way
from stem to stern. The canoe tipped and
bumped, and when it did, Mom most
emphatically told everyone to "sit down or
we'll tip over." No one wanted to tip over in
the Tushmo, of course, for all of the reasons
I explained before, but we really didn't want
to just sit down the whole way either.

Since there was a village at the upper
end of the inlet, other canoes passed us now
and then. They gave us a wide berth as they

went by, as if they thought maybe we'd tip too far and end up in their canoes. Our style didn't inspire confidence, but we did get some big smiles.

Having pretty much run out of paddling room and ways to scare Mom, we turned around and headed for home. We went faster now, even if not much straighter, because we were getting more confident and because it was fun to see how big a bow wave we could make. Water lapped over the sides and a gentle breeze blew our hair and I'm sure Mom wondered why she had ever suggested this.

Suddenly, just as we were about to exit the Tushmo and paddle back into the friendlier waters of the lake, we hit a big log that was hidden just under the surface. It happened so fast that before we knew what hit us, or rather what we hit, the right side of the canoe tipped right down to where water gushed in over the side.

In a desperate effort to stay dry, most of us jumped up. We teetered back and forth and our wet feet thrashed on the slippery bottom of the canoe. Before Mom could yell "SIT DOWN!" we had all fallen into the creepy Tushmo. If ever I had wished to walk on water, that was it, but there was no time

to think about it, what with both the canoe
and Sandy sinking.

"Somebody help Sandy," shouted Mom,
who could stand up in the neck deep water.
I grabbed Sandy and perched on the log that
had dumped us so I wouldn't have to put my
feet down. Terry and Towner emptied the
canoe while Mom waded to shore,
amazingly uneaten by anything.

Mom never got back in. She and Sandy
walked home on a trail and left us three
boys to paddle the canoe back to its dock.

I wish I could say we paddled straight
back as Mom expected. It would have saved
us all a lot of grief, but that isn't what
happened. We couldn't resist the chance to
get a little more practice swamping the
canoe, so we paddled right out into the
middle of the lake, where the wind was
blowing and the waves were high. I suppose
we should have gotten permission first, but
as my dad always said, "It's easier to get
forgiveness than permission."

For the next hour, while our parents and
Towner's parents worried about us, we had
the time of our lives. We tipped the canoe
over every way we could, emptying it in
between dumps. Sometimes while it was
upside down we'd swim underneath it and

hide, breathing the trapped air and making ear piercing screams in the aluminum hull. I suppose it might have looked from a distance that we'd all drowned and the canoe was just floating there.

When we finally heard someone shouting from the high bank a couple hundred yards away, it didn't sound as if they were in a great mood. We could barely make out our four parents' faces as we headed in their direction, and the closer we got, the more unhappy they looked. They obviously hadn't come to welcome us back home.

We tied up the canoe and climbed the steep bank. My Dad's first intelligible words were, "Your goose is cooked." I hadn't ever heard the expression before, but I assumed he wasn't talking about lunch.

Well, we got yelled at and spanked and guilt ridden, but I reckon if you've never done anything worth getting spanked for, you haven't lived. Besides, when I think of all the things my parents let us do in the next few years, I can't for the life of me figure out what was so awful about that hour of fun we had hiding under the canoe in the middle of the lake. I think they were just worried about us, and the only way they could show it was to spank us.

CHAPTER 8

Man of the House

When school got out early in June, 1958, we were raring to get back to the

Machiguengas and their good home cooking. Especially Melody. She was twenty-one months old by then and getting to be a lot of fun. She had cute black curls and probably looked more normal to the Indians than any of the rest of us. She loved to imitate everything the Machiguengas did, including eating her food with just the right fingers and crying exactly like their kids did.

"How soon are we going to the tribe?" I wanted to know.

"Well, we wanted to go right away, but we can't go until we're all over our colds," Mom answered, blowing her nose. The Machis had so few immunities that colds quickly turned into flu and pneumonia, and they died by the dozens.

"Where are we going to stay when we get out there?" Sandy asked. So far we had lived in Timpia, Etariato, Pangoa and Camisea. Machiguenga villages were sprouting all over as the Indians gathered together so they could have schools and access to medicine.

"We're going to go over to the Manu for a while," Dad answered. The Manu River was on a different watershed from the rest of the Machiguenga villages.

All of us, except Melody, sniffled and coughed impatiently at Yarinacocha as the precious days of summer vacation raced past. Mom and I got worse instead of better, and soon had bronchitis. Our flight plans changed each day as our medical prognoses got worse.

About the time Terry started to get better, Melody finally joined in with a blistering hot temperature and a fiery red face. My own fever went higher, making me wonder why they called it a "cold."

Dad finally came up with a major revision in plans. "It looks like Terry and I are going to get better before the rest of you, so why don't we just go out ahead of you all? I'll try to find someone to go with us and we can travel by boat visiting some of the villages downriver until you catch up with us."

I tried every which way to made Dad think I was well enough to go, but the thermometer wouldn't lie and I couldn't stop coughing while I was telling him how good I felt. I was doomed to stay behind.

In the end, Gene Smith the principal of our little school was happy to go with Dad. Since school was out he was glad for the chance to get away from Yarinacocha for a while. His son Terry would go too.

By Friday, June 20th Mom and I were better, but Melody was worse. She came down with diarrhea, which at least provided plenty of stool specimens to give to the lab technician at the clinic. The report said she was loaded with amoeba, which probably came from eating everything the Indians gave her the last time she was out in the tribe, along with a bunch of stuff the Indians didn't give her. Villages aren't very healthy places for little kids who like to pick up whatever they can stick in their mouths.

That afternoon her temperature climbed to 102. She may have had amoeba, but that wasn't the only problem. During the night she shook with chills and sweated with fever, and stated vomiting in the morning. It obviously wasn't a normal cold, but what else could it be? She didn't eat anything all day, and except for times when she was napping, Mom spent the whole day holding her.

Melody hadn't eaten anything but a little ice cream again — the fourth day in a row. She was still running a fever and slept most of the morning on our well-padded dining room table.

"I'm wondering if I should postpone our

flight again, Chica," Dad told Mom using his pet name for her. "I don't feel very good about leaving you and our sick little girl when we're not sure what's wrong with her. I'm not even taking a radio with me, so we won't be able to talk while I'm gone."

Dad planned to take a receiver so he could listen to news from Yarinacocha, but he wouldn't be able to respond. The transmitter and the generator that powered the two-way were just too heavy and bulky for river travel.

"Well, it still just seems like a bad cold or the flu or something like that," Mom reassured him. "I think we'll be all right if she'll just start eating again."

Tuesday morning, to Dad's relief, Melody had a bit of an appetite.

"Well, now that I've seen her eat something I guess I can go happy," he told Mom.

Just before he got on the plane, Dad pulled me aside. "You're going to have to be the man of the house while we're separated," he solemnly told me. "Do your best to help Mom and take good care of Sandy until Melody gets better." I soberly nodded my head to show that I understood. I would rather have been the six-year-old tag-along in the village than the six-year-old "man of the house" at Yarinacocha, but I didn't have much choice.

We watched the plane until it lifted off the lake and shrank into a tiny dot just over the horizon. Then we went back up the hill to our house, where Sandy and Melody and I all had to lie down for a while. The trip to see the plane off had been my first venture out of the house for a couple of weeks.

When Sandy and I got up, Melody was still sleeping in her bed. In a few minutes we heard a noise, and ran to see what had happened.

"Mom, Melody just fell on the floor and she can't get up," I called. Mom thought it was because she'd been carried around so much for five days.

That afternoon Melody got down from her chair to get a cookie she'd dropped. She once again ended up in a heap on the floor. Mom sat down a few feet away, a worried look on her face.

"Melody, can you come to Mommy?" She held out her hands invitingly, but Melody's legs just buckled when she tried to walk.

"Ronny, keep an eye on Sandy," Mom told me with worry in her voice. "I've got to get Melody up to the clinic. Something's wrong with her legs."

Mom scooped her up and headed for the door. Her obvious concern was contagious, and for the first time I was afraid of what might happen to our little sister.

"Has she had her polio shots?" Uncle Doc Eichenberger asked while he checked Melody over.

"She's had the first two, but not the third one yet," Mom answered.

"If it's not polio, it may be a mild form of meningitis," Uncle Doc said thoughtfully after he'd taken a blood sample. "That would be consistent with the five days of fever. Keep her as quiet and comfortable as you can and we'll see how she's doing in the morning. The more she stays flat on her back the better, because it'll minimize any spinal cord irritation."

Waiting was a pain, literally and figuratively. Melody didn't want to stay down, and Mom had a hard time feeding her flat on her back. Besides, Melody was obviously feeling a lot of pain every time she moved. Mom borrowed a baby buggy from friends and took Melody for long rides around the center, just to relieve the boredom.

By Thursday Uncle Doc advised Mom to

bring her to the clinic for more tests. They would start with an X-ray to check for tuberculosis. Depending on the X-rays, they might have to do a spinal tap as well.

The X-ray was at least easy to get. Mom waited while Uncle Doc took the film into the darkroom and developed it himself. When he came out all he said was, "I think we'd better do a spinal tap too."

Melody never took life stoically. Giving her a simple shot would have been a wrestling match, and trying to give her a spinal tap was next to impossible. She thrashed and screamed and it took Mom plus two nurses to hold her down. They had to bend her into a painful position and hold her still and when it was all over the whole fight had been useless. Nothing had come out. Uncle Doc had to give up. While waiting for a syringe to boil, he sat down across the emergency table from Mom.

"I think we have to consider the possibility of tuberculous meningitis," he said. "I found a spot in her lung, not very clear but still there. If that's what we're dealing with, it's extremely urgent that you get her some good help immediately." Polio and meningitis shared some of the same symptoms, since they both attacked the brain and spinal cord, but since Melody had had polio shots, meningitis seemed more likely.

"You should fly to Lima as soon as you can and go directly on to Panama. There's a hospital there that specializes in tropical diseases and Melody will get excellent care. Besides, it's closer than the U.S. and every hour counts."

Mom walked home in a daze. Neighbors and friends rallied to pray, help pack, and make travel reservations for Saturday. Aunt Elaine Townsend, Uncle Cam's wife, came over right in the middle of the mess to help pack, and to hand Mom an envelope full of money for medical bills. Aunt Virginia Smith, Gene's wife, offered to keep Sandy and me.

It all happened so fast that Sandy and I were just kind of fending for ourselves, lost in the whirlwind. We ran errands and tried to help entertain Melody, but there wasn't much we could do for her.

Uncle Doc went to the radio tower and talked to the operator.

"Broadcast a message every once in a while to Wayne Snell telling him to get to a transmitter as soon as possible. If he answers, connect him to my phone immediately." They never got the message.

Thursday night and Friday morning were the worst. Melody cried continuously, in constant pain, her dark ringlets soaked with sweat. I watched her while Mom went to the dining hall to pick up some breakfast for us. When someone asked her how Melody was doing, Mom just burst into tears.

"I think she's getting worse and worse," she cried. "and I don't know if we can get her help in time. She can hardly move without screaming now." Panama City seemed a long way off, and every hour's delay increased the risk of permanent brain damage or death.

When Uncle Doc came that morning to examine Melody, he disagreed with Mom.

"I think she's actually doing a bit better," he said kind of to himself, even though Melody had started screaming again when she saw him coming. We all grew up with a reverence approaching worship of Uncle Doc, one of the world's best authorities on tropical medicine, but at the time Melody thought of him as nothing but a pain in the back.

"It looks to me like whatever it is, it's settling in her right side, and especially in her right leg," he went on. "I'm starting to suspect polio again, although it's really hard to tell without good lab tests. Let's hold off on the trip to Lima for now. I'll give her a skin test so we can really check out the tuberculosis angle and then I'll call to get your reservations cancelled." Mom told Sandy and me the good news that she and Melody wouldn't be leaving.

"Oh well," I answered philosophically, "maybe some other time when you get real sick Aunt Virginia can take care of us." We all liked Aunt Virginia, and not getting to stay with her was a big disappointment. Besides, it would've been nice to just eat some real meals at home with someone.

Polio would be a big relief compared to meningitis, especially since it didn't seem to be advancing any further. As Uncle Doc told us, "If we could choose between meningitis and polio, I'd sure take the polio." Even so, there was a good possibility of paralysis, especially in Melody's legs.

By the next week, it was clear that she could at least move everything — toes, arms, legs and head. She started getting hot soaks for her legs, and they slowly came back to life, although for a couple more weeks she pretty much stayed on our dining table where she could see everything that was going on.

Mom and I took turns watching her so she wouldn't roll off, and I sort of made sure that we all got fed. Usually I took Sandy to our group dining hall for breakfast, lunch and supper. After we'd eaten, I carried a plate home for Mom, who seldom left Melody for more than a few minutes. Although it only lasted about three weeks, I got tired of eating alone, tired of carrying the laundry over to the laundromat, tired of being "the man of the house."

Our neighbors and friends all pitched in to help like one big family. Their concern was heart-warming. In the end, Mom returned a lot of the money that had been donated because the whole clinic bill had come to just over $20.00.

By the time Dad got the news and flew back to Yarinacocha, the crisis was over. A couple days later, he once again pulled me aside.

"Mommy says she doesn't know how she would have survived without your help. She says you've done way more than your share to take care of her and Melody and Sandy. I want to give you a little gift to show you how thankful I am."

I didn't feel that I'd been a very good "man of the house," but he gave me a brand new handsaw with six interchangeable blades. I was very proud of it, but forgot it under a mango tree one of the first times I used it. By the time I found it again the blades had all rusted into one.

In the end, it really was polio, and the muscles in Melody's legs were seriously affected. She walked with braces for a while, then began a series of corrective surgeries that have left her walking almost normally. With her determination, her legs have seldom slowed her down.

"They say" Melody probably got the polio from the daughter of a Machiguenga friend. We didn't know until much later that there were many children in the area who had polio that year.

"They say" Melody was lucky to have had two shots already, since that probably minimized the damage.

"They say" we should be very grateful that we had colds in June, or we would have all been in the middle of nowhere, far from medical help of any sort when our sister got sick.

We are.

CHAPTER 9

Spam Stampede

It was just before dark in Camisea. We had finished bathing in the river, where bare bottomed kids splashed in the shallows and older women squatted down to peel off their cushma robes and scooch modestly into the water.

The tiny gnats that swarmed in clouds along the river banks and tortured us endlessly during the day had all gone home to bed. For a while we could stop swatting and scratching like monkeys with fleas. We had splashed and porpoised and drifted with the current and watched the black bats take over the sky, zigzagging after their favorite insects.

Now, the smell of campfire smoke drifted over the airstrip where we played ball as the sun set. In thatched huts around us, manioc, bananas and fish were boiling, roasting and smoking for supper. A cool, peaceful end to a hot summer day. Venus, evening star for now, glittered downriver.

Suddenly a ten-year-old girl burst into the village as if she'd just seen her father's spirit. She and her mother had gone to fill their gourds with water from a small creek that emptied into the river just up from us.

"Pigs are coming. They're crossing the river," she panted through split palm walls on her way past. "Lots of them." Her homespun striped cotton robe whipped around her skinny legs as she ran.

Men exploded from their huts like popcorn, grabbing shotguns and bows and arrows. Darkness was coming fast now, and

Machiguengas were terrified of the spirits that ran wild in the dark. Still, the chance to have fresh pig meat delivered right to their doors was too good to miss.

Wild pig is a favorite meat for the Machiguengas. Besides, the skins sold for enough money downriver to make them worth collecting and preserving. Good hunters went to great pains to kill the pigs without damaging the hides. The best pig hunter we knew, Pascual, sometimes sneaked up so close that he could just whack a pig on the top of the head with a club. For Terry and me, at eleven and ten, that was an awesome feat.

In fact, for Terry and me killing a pig any which way was an awesome feat, and we didn't care if the pig didn't even have a hide by the time we were done. We weren't quite as desperate for the two bucks the skin would fetch, and we weren't about to go crawling up to a pig and whang it on the head, even if we could have.

"Dad, can we go with them?" We were already well on our way. An army of wild parents couldn't have kept us away from a herd of white lipped peccaries stampeding right in our own back yard. Hunting their cousins, the white collared peccaries, was tedious and tame by comparison. It took hours of visiting their favorite mudholes, following their tracks, stealthily getting within shooting range, and whispering the whole time.

White lipped peccaries ran in herds of up to 500 and traveled long distances each day. When they came through, the whole jungle jumped out of their way, since they didn't give a whole lot of thought to going around anything they could knock over, including hunters. Hunting them didn't have a thing to do with stalking and whispering. It was more like being at a football game with everyone yelling and the pigskins running the plays.

Navidad, one of our closest neighbors and one of the village's better hunters, wasn't so sure we should go.

"It's getting dark and the pigs can be pretty dangerous when they stampede like this. Teri and Rani might get killed," he told my dad. The possibility of us getting killed seemed to bother him more than it did us or Dad.

"None of the other kids are going," Navidad continued. Presumably that was because their parents loved them and told them not to. Dangers aside, it was also obvious that Navidad didn't think we'd be much help.

"Just get your shoes on and do what they tell you." Dad knew the Machiguengas probably wouldn't let the pigs run over us. Ever since we were tiny babies they had gone to great pains, sometimes literally, to make sure we survived our own stupidity.

It seemed unfair that we had to put shoes on when the Machiguengas got to go barefoot, but this was no time to argue. We backtracked to our house, grabbed dirty canvas tennis shoes and hopped off on alternate legs as we tied them on. We didn't want to be left behind.

In the dusky half light we all ran the gauntlet through two rows of thatched huts. Women and children laughed as our white skins flashed past the cracks in their walls. Beyond the houses the trail wound through a small garden where papayas, bananas, cassava and sweet potatoes grew. Then we rushed ten minutes off into the jungle. It was all Terry and I could do to keep up, crashing around trees and through the undergrowth, trying to miss the stickery palm trees with their spiked trunks.

There was no doubt that there were a lot of pigs close by. We could all hear them thundering through the jungle. Too late, I wondered if maybe we shouldn't have come after all, but by now we couldn't turn back.

"Quick, climb a tree," Navidad ordered as the sounds of running hooves got heart poundingly close. In an adrenaline rush, Terry and I jumped for the nearest trees and shinnied like white-bellied spider monkeys. This was no time to be choosy about which trees to climb. All we cared about was getting every chewable part of ourselves higher than a pig could reach. Meanwhile, Navidad balanced himself on a skinny log that made a bridge over a V-shaped gulley. Pretty brave, we thought, as dozens of pigs roared underneath him. Just one small slip and he'd return to the dust of the earth.

We heard a loud blast, then a grunt. Another blast and a squeal. Navidad shot down at the pigs that ran underneath him, teetering back and forth at the gun's recoil. There was no point in aiming, since by now it was too dark to see the pigs. Shotgun shells were precious, but pigs were delicious. Blind luck would have to do.

Terry and I weren't having fun. As I said, when we headed up our trees, we were too panicked to care what kind of trees we were climbing. Now that we had time to collect our breath, we both realized we were in thorn trees, and if there's one thing less fun than hugging a pin cushion, it's hugging pins. About the best thing you could say for it was that we weren't in danger of sliding down. Sliding down, as a matter of fact, would have left most of us stuck to the trees.

To add to our problems, every climbable tree in the jungle has ants in it, and these ants were overjoyed to find us on their doorstep so late in the day. Kind of like we'd been overjoyed to have pigs on our doorstep so late in the day. The ants bit and the thorns poked and it was too dark to see anything from our ringside seats. If only we had listened to Navidad instead of Dad.

"Boom." "Kablam." Noise everywhere. Pigs bellowed, screamed and clacked their teeth. The hunters laughed and joked as Machis do when they're really scared. Terry and I grunted and squealed as we tried to find more comfortable positions on the thorns. For ten or fifteen minutes it was blind chaos. Hundreds of pigs churned under and around us.

Suddenly it was over. Deafening silence. The spam stampede had passed. Neither Terry nor I had seen a pig the whole time.

"Are you there?" Navidad called out, and seemed a bit relieved when we answered that we were, indeed, still there. "Let's go," he said, and waited for us to work our way tenderly back to the ground. He mercifully didn't say anything about our choice of trees, but by the time morning came we knew the village would be full of laughs about how we had both climbed sticker trees. They loved to tell stories about how helpless we were, and we might even get nicknames to remind everyone of our most recent incompetence.

After all that, we couldn't see any dead pigs to lug home.

"Didn't you kill any?" we asked Navidad.

"I don't know yet," he answered. "It's too dark to see. I think I shot a couple, but I'll have to come back in the morning and look for them."

"Oh good, we'll come help you," we offered eagerly. We could tell by his reaction that we'd have to get up early or he'd sneak off without us. With us to help him, it would take twice as long.

More slowly this time, we picked our way back to the village, following right behind Navidad's dark shape. He was glad for our company now, because if the "whistling ones" caught him alone in the jungle at night they would break him up inside and he would die. Not as wary of the spirit world that was such a vivid part of Navidad's life, Terry and I were just afraid of getting lost if we didn't keep up.

The next morning, to our amazement and joy, Navidad actually came to get us.

"Tsame," he said, and off we went.

The sun was barely up and a damp dawn fog still hung low in the tree tops. Just to be sure we wouldn't miss out, Terry and I had already done our morning chores, carrying buckets of water from the river and using a turkey feather fan to bring our log fire to life so we could boil drinking water for the day.

With Dad's long old semi-automatic .22 rifle over Terry's shoulder, we retraced our previous night's trail, following Navidad and his 12 gauge shotgun between the houses, through the gardens, back into the jungle. In the distance, a family of hairy red howler monkeys roared their morning calls. Dew dripped off the trees and highlighted freshly spun spider webs. Pairs of blue and gold macaws squawked high above us. Navidad slid quickly through the jungle. We tromped behind him, about as stealthy as two chain saws.

By the time we got back to the thorn trees and log bridge, Navidad had slowed considerably. He bent over, checking the ground and scanning the undergrowth. Wild pigs can be vicious when they're wounded, and their inch and a half long tusks make rather deep furrows in legs and arms. Terry and I kept climbable trees in sight, just in case a wounded pig surprised us.

"His blood," Navidad showed us at last without much commentary. We would have to track the wounded pig. Rather, Navidad would have to track the pig, and we would have to follow Navidad. We weren't much in the way of pig trackers unless the pig had a leash.

It was slow going. A blood drop here, hoof marks there, broken plants along the way. Disturbed leaves on the ground. Navidad even stooped occasionally to smell plants, his nose searching for directions. White lipped peccaries' strong, peculiar smell lingers on the plants they touch. When all signs of the pig's trail eventually petered out in a dry stream bed, we searched in every direction.

"*Neri.*" Navidad whispered as he pointed with his lips. "He's over there." Sure enough, at the top of the far bank, the wounded pig lay almost hidden in the leaves. Quietly and even more cautiously now, we stalked closer. Navidad raised his shotgun to his shoulder. The pig, obviously smelling us about as easily as we could smell him, stood up and the stiff hair on his back bristled. He clacked his teeth as if it would scare us. It did.

Terry got the .22 off his shoulder and removed the safety catch. The hair on his neck bristled just like the pig's, mostly because in those days Dad cut our hair. Not that the pig would know the difference.

The pig was mostly black, with a white chin and throat as if he hadn't gotten his shaving cream rinsed off. His head was big, tapering from large jowls to a narrow pink disk of a nose about the size of a quarter. Long tusks made scary lumps under his top lips. His tiny red eyes glared at us, daring us to come a little closer. The shotgun blast from the night before had hit him broadside.

"Look, his guts are bulging out," I whispered, staring at the bloody pink ball hanging in front of the pig's back leg.

"Shhh!" Terry was getting ready for a shot and obviously didn't want to be reminded that this ferocious pig was already half dead.

"Blam!" In the quiet of the jungle Navidad's gun blast echoed several seconds after it made a ragged hole in the pig's shoulder. The pig lurched. So did we. Navidad spread one arm out to keep us back, as if he thought we might just rush in for a look.

"*Tsikyanira*," Navidad said, as if we didn't already know to be careful. With a big hole in its side from the night before, and a fresh hole in its shoulder, the pig was rather dead by this time. Still it wouldn't do to have one of our hands in its mouth when it went into its final convulsions, and Navidad knew very well that we just might attempt something that dumb.

Dead or not, the pig was still on its legs, which was really lucky for Terry, who desperately wanted to help kill it. I could almost hear him muttering to himself, "Hang on, baby, you can do it — don't fall down yet."

His first shot hit the pig smack in the jaw, setting off another involuntary wave of clacking and rattling that the pig probably didn't even know about. Navidad was quietly laughing, the back of his hand

discreetly covering his mouth. Milliseconds
flew past. The rifle had instantly reloaded
itself, so there might still be time for
another shot before the pig fell down.

Terry didn't even pause to enjoy his first
hit before he fired another bullet that hit
the pig's ear. That did it. Even with instant
reloading there was no time left, and a dead
pig can only stand up for so long. Down it
tumbled, gaining speed as it rolled into the
dry stream bed.

We slid down after it for a closer look. It
didn't take a hide dealer to tell us that this
pig's skin wasn't going to be worth much.
Two shotgun blasts and two .22 shells had
pretty much reduced the potential leather
to wallet size.

Hide aside, the meat was still good, so we
cleaned out what was left of the guts and
bundled the carcass to carry home. First
Navidad cut a vine to tie the legs together,
then a wide strip of bark to make a head
strap. Finally he got a bunch of broad soft
leaves to put between the pig and his back
to keep both ticks and bristles off his bare
skin.

When Navidad wasn't looking, Terry
and I wiped fresh blood on our clothes and
arms so everyone could see what mighty

hunters we were. This was a proud moment, and we were heady with our success. It didn't matter a bit that Terry had shot the pig after it was already dead and I hadn't shot it at all.

We helped hoist the pig and hold it while Navidad got the head strap adjusted just right, and then walked proudly back into the village. Navidad was doing the work, but we were quite sure that all the girls would know that his success was due solely to our help. We split up at the airstrip. Navidad took the pig on over to his house for skinning and butchering, and we went home for breakfast.

About an hour later Navidad's shy eleven-year-old daughter, Carmen, came over with one of the pig's front legs on a chipped enamel plate. It would be normal to share game all around the village, but it looked as if we got one of the best pieces in recognition of our invaluable contribution to the hunt. Carmen kind of glanced at Terry and me out of the corners of her eyes while she handed Mom the meat. Then she buried her face in her robe and ran off giggling. It was pretty clear she'd just heard the whole story.

CHAPTER 10

Yellow Brother, Yellow Mother

Shironkama wasn't a particularly good role model. He was a fierce, rugged man, with a tiger tooth carved to fit into his top gum where one of his own teeth had rotted out. He was bald, rare among the Machis, so he always, always wore a tattered cap to avoid being called "gourd head." His face looked like an unfinished mahogany wood carving, still waiting for the final touches to make it handsome.

Shironkama had a lot more power than most Machis, but he had gotten it by capturing his fellow Machiguengas and turning them over to rubber companies as slaves. When other influencial Machiguengas got in his way, he used his authority, meaning the gun he got from the rubber companies, to kill them. To put it bluntly, he was a murderer, thief and slave trader. I thought he was really cool.

When we first met powerful Shironkama, we were living in our very first house in Timpia and he was lying powerless in the bottom of a canoe, dying of diarrhea. The slaves who brought him to us had poled and paddled his canoe all the way up from the Picha River, a full week's trip, hoping that Dad and Mom could give him some medicine. They did, and Shironkama became a grateful friend, calling my parents "Father" and "Mother" for the rest of his life. He was a dutiful "son" to them, a special "brother" to me. Every year after they saved his life, he made the long trip to visit us wherever we happened to be living at the time, bringing gifts and trade goods.

The second time Shironkama visited us we were still living in Timpia, and he had just heard about the school that was starting there. Although he already had a lot of power around Picha because of his ruthless reputation, he had been told that if he learned to read and write he would be able to sit at a desk and tell people what to do. That was too good to pass up, so he asked Dad if he could get a school started at Picha, like the one at Timpia.

Dad started with the basics.

"How many students do you have?"

"My family and my slaves."

"Before you can have a school you have to have at least 20 students. Go get some people together and then we'll send a teacher." Traditionally the Machiguengas lived in small isolated family groups rather than in villages.

"*Nani*," Shironkama agreed. Then before he left to return to Picha he tried to show his gratitude.

"Here, you can have Olivia. All I want is a machete for her." Thirteen-year-old Olivia trembled at the thought of being Shironkama's way of saying thanks to Dad, but she didn't have much choice. Shironkama barked out orders telling her what he expected of her as the gringo's slave. Fortunately, Dad didn't need another slave since he already had Mom and Terry and me.

"We don't want her." Hopefully Olivia wouldn't take it personally.

"Keep her anyway."

"Okay, she can stay and help us, but we'll pay for her help and we'll send her back to you later."

Shironkama returned downriver to Picha, assured that if he got enough students together, he would get a school.

The next year when he returned, we and the school were moving to Etariato. In fact, it was Shironkama and his slaves who did us the favor of dumping all our belongings off the raft into the Pongo between Pangoa and Etariato when we moved.

"I have about twenty students ready for school at Picha," Shironkama reported. "Can you give us a teacher now?"

No one asked how he had gotten so many people to move together so quickly. Many of the children, it turned out, were orphans.

True to his word, Dad asked Abelino to be the first teacher at Picha, but he didn't last long. He developed tuberculosis and was too much of a tightwad to spend any of his precious teacher's pay on the expensive medicine. Still, he earned the people's respect by sticking with them in the school until his last breath.

After Abelino died, Mario replaced him in the Picha school. It was Mario's first teaching position, but in his crazy way he soon had all of the school kids in the palm of his hand. In fact, about twenty of them lived in his own house — the Picha version of a children's home. He was about fifteen, with a squashed flat nose, tattoos on his face, wildly bowed legs and a total height of about 4' 10". He looked like a miniature brown cowboy that had just been thrown face first into the side of a barn. He was always full of energy and ideas. In Timpia and Etariato he used to play with us in the river. No matter how hard we tried, we could never drown him.

Mario was as independent and feisty as any Machi ever was, and even as a teenager he would stand up to Shironkama. As a matter of fact, he later stole one of Shironkama's slave girls for a wife. Rather than shoot him, Shironkama asked my dad to intervene. After several hours of talking back and forth, Mario still had his wife. He was one of my heroes, and I loved him like a big brother.

Through the next few years Dad and Mom both visited Picha briefly, but we had never lived there as a family. Shironkama repeatedly begged us to come, wanting advice on the school, medical help for the people and teaching from the Scripture portions that my parents had translated so far.

Finally, it looked as if we were going to get to spend a few months at Picha. When school got out in 1959, we flew right out to Camisea, planning to spend a few weeks there before we moved to Picha.

On June 29th, the day Terry turned nine, he turned yellow.

Since yellow wasn't his normal color, his complexion worried Dad and Mom, even though it was kind of fun for us to stare at. Yellow eyeballs, yellow skin, dark brownish yellow urine (he said). He was so tired he didn't even want to get out of bed to celebrate.

"Terremoto, wake up, Son. Happy birthday!" Dad wanted him to join us for breakfast, which Terry wasn't enthusiastic about. After breakfast Dad and Mom gave

him a whopping two bucks and nine balloons and his own box of fudge. He felt so awful I wondered if maybe I'd get the fudge, but I couldn't say anything just yet.

After a long day of lying around doing nothing, Terry didn't even eat his special birthday supper of smoked fish and boiled manioc. For dessert we had chocolate cake baked in a frying pan over hot coals. Mom lit it up with candles and we all tried to celebrate. In the yellow candlelight, Terry looked even yellower. Since he didn't want any cake, it was time to assume something was drastically wrong.

The next day Terry was genuinely sick, there was a worm making its painful home in my right foot, and Mom was taking sulpha tablets to fight off some diarrhea. To top it off, all our stuff was in a mess as we sorted and packed for our move to Picha. It seemed, sometimes, as if our whole lives were in a mess.

Thursday morning, with the plane already on its way to take us to Picha, Dad decided it was time to consult the Doctor at Yarinacocha.

"Yarina, this is Camisea, do you copy us? Over."

"Roger, Camisea, you're coming in

nicely. What can we do for you? Over."

"We've got a sick boy on our hands and need to talk to Doc. Can you set us up with a sched? Over"

"Wayne, stand by a minute while I try to reach him."

"Roger, we're standing by." We waited while the radio operator tried to reach Doc.

"Camisea," he finally replied, "we can't get ahold of Doc. Corny Hibbard just had her baby and he's at the clinic with her. Do you want me to keep trying? Over."

"No," Dad answered with a hint of frustration. "We're expecting the plane any time and we've got to get our radio down. We'll check back when we get an antenna up in Picha. Thanks anyway. Over and out."

Uncle George Insley landed the little Aeronca float plane in front of our house around two o'clock and helped cram Mom, Sandy and Melody in with a load of baggage for the first twenty-minute flight.

Things weren't any better in Picha. When Mom and the girls landed, all of the men were gone except for a couple of frightened "long hairs," the most primitive of the Machiguengas. They weren't about to get close to the plane, so Mom and Uncle George unloaded it themselves. Then while

Mom and the girls started cleaning out the house and hanging mosquito nets, Uncle George came back for us.

While the plane was making that trip, Terry just lay on the porch in a yellow haze and I hobbled around on one foot. When it finally came back to get us, we painfully helped Dad and Uncle George cram in another huge load of baggage and ourselves on top of it.

Our ears popped as we lopsidedly broke free of the water on the first try.

"Hey, we did it!" Uncle George yelled with a big smile, patting the instrument panel affectionately. At least that's probably what he yelled. It was a little hard to tell over the noise of the engine. Talking to each other in a Knocker was like a conversation between two people who were hard of hearing. It involved a lot of yelling, a lot of saying "Uh huh" to questions you couldn't hear, and lip reading. Unfortunately, when you're sitting behind the pilot it's hard to read his lips.

"How's everybody doing back there?"

"Uh huh," Terry and I said.

"Are you comfortable?"

"About two months, if possible," Dad answered.

"Ol' Terry's not feeling so good, huh?"

"We've got some sandwiches. We'll be all right." And so it went.

A cool refreshing wind blasted in the vent holes and we relaxed as we wound our way between fluffy white clouds.

Landing was almost as fun as taking off. When the floats first hit the water, they danced along like a skipping stone until the pilot cut the engine and we settled down in the water to taxi to shore.

Within fifteen minutes an unbelievable assortment of stuff appeared out of the little airplane like rabbits out of a magician's hat. Several Machiguenga men arrived back from a canoe trip downriver just as we were unloading, and they were thrilled to get in on part of this magnificent show.

"*Pokakevi?*" The typical Machiguenga greeting seemed a rather obvious question. "You've come?" Out of courtesy every cushma-clad resident had to ask everyone who'd just arrived, presumably to ensure that everyone who seemed to be standing there really was.

"I've come," I answered dozens of times. In between swatting gnats and responding to greetings and limping in the sand, I helped get the radio set up on the beach so

Dad could call Yarina again.

"Yarina, this is Wayne Snell and we've all just arrived at Picha. What are chances of getting ahold of Doc now? Over."

"Roger, Picha, we'll get him. Stand by."

In a few moments Uncle Doc's raspy voice asked some diagnostic questions and told Dad how to feel Terry's liver for possible enlargement. It didn't take long to come up with a verdict.

"Sounds to me like hepatitis. I think George should spend the night out there and bring Terry in with him tomorrow. There's not much you can do for him, and he can stay with us until he's over it." Doc hadn't even bothered to ask Aunt Beth, his wife, if that was all right. He just assumed that she wouldn't mind a third boy in the house. Even a yellow one.

We kids liked Yarinacocha, and Phil and Mark Eichenberger were just like brothers, but living in the tribe for the summers was our piece of paradise. To have to go back to Yarina just when he'd got out there was about like getting three months of detention for Terry. Even a promise that he could take his puppy with him wasn't much of a consolation.

Sadly we headed for the house the

Indians had cleaned out for us. In their enthusiasm to have us there, the small community had gone to great lengths to make sure that once we arrived we would be able to actually get to our house. They had graciously cut dozens of steps into the clay so Mom could go back and forth to the river, carrying nothing more than herself and even so clutching a helpful brown arm for support.

Since teacher Mario had lived near us in both Timpia and Etariato years before, he still had vivid memories of watching Don Juan haul Mom bodily up the bank. He was the one who had suggested steps.

Helpful men hoisted boxes, bags and sacks to their shoulders and carried them up for us. The house we headed for had the usual pona floor two feet off the ground and a thatched roof made of thousands of special palm leaves, neatly folded and interlaced. About a hundred crickets and a family of bats lived in our roof.

There were no walls. Six thick logs buried deep in the ground held up the floor and roof. Of course the whole house was tied together with vines. A notched log got us from the ground to the floor. Within minutes the whole place was chaotic confusion. Our supplies were scattered all over the floor. Curious Indians by the dozens crowded around just to watch, since admission was free. Thursday afternoon at the matinee.

By the time it was dark, we were ready for the night. Air mattresses were inflated, mosquito nets up, drinking water boiled on our log fire. Crackers and a can of tuna fish would hold us over until we could get organized. Dessert was one malted milk ball apiece — a special treat a friend in Yarinacocha had sent on the plane. We went to bed, all on the floor, all in a row.

The next morning we got up early to get Terry and Uncle George off in the Knocker. Over the radio, Uncle Doc assured us that they were ready and waiting. It wasn't a happy morning for any of us, winding single file down to the plane like part of a funeral procession. It didn't take any time at all to load Terry, the dog and his little bag of stuff, and then we all waved goodbye as the Aeronca taxied out into the river and lifted off. Yellow tears ran down Terry's yellow face as he looked out the window of the yellow plane.

The next couple of days were full. When I wasn't playing I worked with my parents tying together shelves, sorting boxes and cans, setting up a rough counter for the primus stove and keeping our cook fire going. Neighbors came with woven mats to tie around part of the house so the wind wouldn't blow everything off our porch.

By Sunday things were finally taking shape. After church in the school house, I took five-year-old Sandy and three-year-old Melody down to the river to swim with Mario's pet tapir while Dad and Mom went for a walk in the jungle. I'm sure what Mom really wanted to do was eat malted milk balls without having to share.

On the walk Mom started feeling weird. She and Dad were looking at purple passion flowers that grew wild around the village. Her malted milk balls weren't going down too well, which for Mom is a little like going to paradise and suddenly coming to the awful conclusion that you can't stand it.

By Monday she had aching joints and a high fever that aspirin couldn't bring down. Tuesday was worse, but she struggled along, trying to bring a little order into the remaining mess around us. An epidemic of flu had just hit the tribal area, and everyone assumed that's what it was.

Dark, drippy Wednesday was an

ominous day. Mom was sick to her stomach, irritable and increasingly depressed, lying for long stretches on her floor mat. It rained all day. Our whole world was socked in and soaked with clouds, drizzle and blowing mist. The only way to get anywhere was to wade through puddles and along muddy trails. The roof over the flimsy outhouse leaked, soaking the toilet paper and making our already slippery squatting boards pretty risky. Our little enamel potty was getting a lot of good use.

Night came early under the black clouds and we went to bed by eight o'clock, as usual laid out side by side on the floor along one wall, with me closest to the front of the house. Rain drip drip dripped off the roof. Under most circumstances it was a sound we loved — a cozy sound that put us right to sleep curled up under our blankets.

That night I lay awake longer than usual. We were all used to being sick, but Mom looked really bad and we were a long way from help. A plane would never be able to come after us if the blowing rain kept up. Our stuff was still mostly in boxes and food was hard to fix. The only difference between this and camping out was that camping out was fun.

Tossing and turning in my white mosquito net, I could hear our neighbors quietly muttering to each other, clearing their throats to spit, or getting up to go to the bushes. They didn't have enamel potties. Their palm floors, like ours, creaked and bounced as they walked. Dogs barked and growled. Babies cried. Crickets chirped in the roof. The smell of dying cook fires drifted through the house. Fruit bats fluttered in the rafters. Eventually I drifted off to sleep surrounded by the familiar sounds of home.

Suddenly there was a loud, splintering crack followed by a heavy crash, as if a tree had just fallen in or on our house. This wasn't one of the familiar sounds of home. Flashlights clicked on, groggy eyes tried to focus.

"Daddy," Sandy said drousily, "The roof just fell down." Then she went back to sleep as if it happened all the time. Dad and I took a closer look.

She was right. The day's rain had soaked into the thatch, weighing it down. The right front house pole, already old and tired, split under the heavy load. The whole front corner of our roof sat on our porch in a clutter of torn palm leaves. It seemed an awful time to have our roof fall in, with Mom sick and all.

"What if the rest of it falls down?" I asked. We were, after all, sleeping under it.

"I think it'll be all right. Let's go back to bed." There wasn't anything we could do about it anyway.

Thursday morning our house went from bad to awful. Our still-scattered stuff was covered with bits of leaves. The Indians came to begin repairs, taking apart broken sections and hauling in new logs, vines and leaves. Dad started the generator that powered our huge radio and yelled into it as he talked to Yarinacocha.

Reception was poor, but it wouldn't have mattered if it had been excellent — Dad just yelled into radios, as if he didn't really trust wireless connections. In the midst of it all, Mom lay in the back of the noisy, bouncing, cluttered, shaking house, rapidly getting worse and worse.

Dad asked to talk to Dr. Eichenberger, and luckily got right through.

"Doc, we're thinking Betty might have hepatitis too. She's not yellow yet, but she's pretty nauseated and has a high fever and her right side is quite tender. Any chance you could come out on the plane and look her over?"

Uncle Doc shook his head invisibly over the radio. "If she's crackle sputter crackle sick, you'd better just *oooooeeeeeeoooooo kesshhkkkiiiooooeeee* right away. She's going to need some *craccke pop kkkssshhhh* for a while. How copy so far?"

"Loud and clear," Dad shouted. Anything intelligible was considered loud and clear, and we were all experts at filling in the blanks. "We'll get her there as soon as we can."

"I'll get things *crraaaccckkkkk* this end." Uncle Doc had had hepatitis himself a few years before, and knew just what to expect emotionally and physically. Except that he didn't know that Mom would be much worse than he expected.

Numbly we all scurried to pack up the things we had just unpacked, and worried through the night, roofless. Disappointment hung over the whole village. We had just come. We were already leaving.

It was a confusing and exhausting day. Since the Catalina flying boat was going to be in the area with visitors anyway, passengers were juggled and shuttled back and forth between villages.

Mom was stuck in Picha most of the day

without food, water or a radio. By the time the Aeronca finally came to get her in the afternoon, she had given up hope and was deliriously imagining that she'd been abandoned to die in the village. She barely made it to the plane and almost couldn't get in. Worse yet was the transfer from the Aeronca, across the beach and up into the Catalina's high bubble door.

"I don't think I can make it," she whispered as she looked up the wobbly aluminum ladder.

Strong pilots' arms reached down to pull her up, and one pilot got his head under her backside to push. She toppled into the hull and collapsed on an aluminum bench. Someone handed her a cup of chicken broth. She was getting yellow fast.

The rest of us climbed in and we bounced off the rocks to settle into the churning river.

Our return to Yarinacocha was a long two hours in the Catalina, and it was late in the afternoon by the time we finally touched down on the lake. When we first hit the water, it sounded like gravel spraying against the aluminum hull. Flying water completely covered the bubble windows and dripped in through cracks as we slowed

down. We taxied to a long concrete ramp
and roared up it, both engines at full power,
to park beside the hangar.

The bouncy Burma Jeep got Mom to a
room in the Eichenbergers' house. Uncle
Doc had figured she'd just be there for a
couple of hours while we cleaned out our
house and made the beds. When he actually
saw how quickly she was deteriorating, he
immediately asked a pilot to fly him to
Pucallpa for some IV supplies. He got back
as the sun set, started the IV and stood by.

Along the way, in bits and pieces, we
heard the bad news.

"Hepatitis is a virus that attacks your
liver. When your liver quits working," Uncle
Doc explained, "poisons stay in your body
and they're what make you so sick and so
yellow. They also make you feel despondent
and desperate. Your Mom isn't going to
want people around and she'll get upset
about all kinds of things. For a long time,
she'll feel like all she wants to do is die."

"Is she going to die?" The unanswerable
question on four kids' minds.

"Will there be permanent damage to her
liver?" We knew of missionaries who had
never really recovered from hepatitis and
had to leave the field.

"We'll just have to wait, and pray, and see," Dad answered. Uncle Doc wasn't God.

In church on Sunday morning, Uncle Doc urged everyone to pray. He had never seen anyone live through a case as severe as this one, and the only treatment was rest and a strict diet that prohibited, among other things, greasy foods.

It was the end of July before Dad could relax enough to reassure my grandparents in the U.S. Terry had made a full recovery, I had mostly recovered from a very mild case, and Mom was slowly improving. She could sit up for fifteen minutes a day and eat real food, even though she still had nurses watching her 24 hours a day.

Mom spent two months pretty much flat in bed, first at Eichenbergers' and then at the clinic.

I remember the first time we all got to go visit her at the clinic. Dad, who had a hard time expressing his emotions, said in a kind of husky voice,

"You know, I was really afraid we were going to lose your Mommy girl."

Without God's help, we would have, so we paused to thank him for caring.

After nearly a year of limited activity, Mom made a complete recovery, except that

ever since the hepatitis she's had severe,
physiologically induced panic attacks
whenever she flies. Given our lifestyle,
that's been a high price to pay.

CHAPTER 11

Bats & Rats & Status Symbols

When Terry got bitten by the vampire bat, I was green with envy.

That summer we were living on the Camisea River. I suppose I must have been about eight, and we were having the time of our lives. Just upriver from us there was a turbulent rapid, but right in front of the village we had a huge sandy beach and a long backwater where we could swim, canoe and build sand huts to our hearts' content.

Luckily for us, just after we arrived in June a Machiguenga from upriver floated down to see us in a disposable canoe. To make it he had cut down a special kind of palm tree that had a tall straight trunk with a big bulge in the middle of it, exactly like you'd picture a huge snake that had just swallowed an alligator.

It was pretty easy to cut out the section with the bulge in it, hack open one side, dig out the soft spongy stuff inside and float off downriver.

Of course the little makeshift canoe. weighed about a ton and would only hold two little boys, but we didn't care, and we spent hours paddling and poling it up and down our little section of waterfront.

On day after another unsuccessful fishing trip in our canoe we decided to see if we could spend the night on the beach.

"Dad, can Terry and I camp out on the playa tonight? We'll cook our own supper and everything."

"Sure. Just make sure you take some mosquito nets and stay inside them while you're sleeping." Elated, we headed for the sandbar with our arms full of mosquito nets, cook pot, frying pan, blankets, bananas, crackers, popcorn, turtle eggs and about a hundred other "essentials." It took several trips, so it was a good thing we were within sight of the house.

"I'll build the fire while you put up the mosquito nets," Terry told me. Building the fire was always the fun part.

"No, let's both build the fire and we'll each put up our own nets." I was a year younger than him, but I was onto his tricks. I headed off to gather driftwood while he shaved kindling. Then he got a tiny flame going and we took turns blowing on it the way the Indians did.

Once the fire was going we put up the nets.

"How are we going to hold them up?" I wondered out loud. There wasn't anything nearby to tie them to.

"Oh, let's just push sticks into the sand." Terry suggested. "They'll stay up for one night."

By the time we had organized our considerable gear, most of which we wouldn't have needed in two months, much less an overnight, it was time to cook supper. Sandy, who was four or five and never wanted to be left out of anything, had walked down to squat beside the fire and watch us. The Machiguengas just watched from their houses. They got a big kick out of us going to so much trouble to spend the night 200 yards from a perfectly good house, but then we did a lot of things they couldn't figure out

Terry brought three big rocks over to set the frying pan on, and I poured in some cooking oil. It took a little work, but we finally got our rubbery turtle egg shells torn open and our turtle eggs mostly in the pan. Just about the time they started to sizzle and spatter and smell really good, the fire jumped into the pan, immediately turning both the pan and our turtle eggs into a blazing torch. We rushed to find something to grab the pan with so we could get it off the fire, then blew on it until the fire went out and all that was left in the pan was the barely recognizable black eggs.

"Here, Sandy, you can have them," I offered generously, and she wolfed them down, thrilled to get to be a part of our campout.

We went to bed early, but losing our turtle eggs left us a little hungry, even with the standby crackers and popcorn, so we fanned up the fire in the middle of the night

to boil some cooking bananas. We'd just
gone back to sleep when Terry woke me up.

"Pandy just knocked my mosquito net
down. Can I get in with you?" Pandy was
our little puppy, and he probably knocked
the net down by breathing on it. The way
we put our nets up, if we had at least one
mosquito net still standing in the morning
we considered our night a giant success. We
checked our fish lines, which were still
empty, and went back to bed crowded
together.

The mosquito nets were pretty essential.
For one thing, rumor had it they would
deter jaguars and ocelots. The Machiguengas told stories of waking up in the
morning to find jaguar tracks all around
their nets. Whether or not the stories were
true, they did give us enough of a sense of
security to fall asleep at night, so we used
the nets and wouldn't have considered
camping out without them.

Since we didn't have mosquitoes in that
area, about the only other thing the nets did
was keep out vampire bats. They weren't
even good for that if you didn't stay inside
them, and Terry was a thrasher.

That's why we woke up the next morning
to find Terry had blood all over his face and

a puddle of it on his pillow. In his sleep he'd stuck his head out and a bat took the bait. Since bats inject a bit of anesthetic and an anticoagulant when they bite, Terry hadn't felt anything from start to finish, and he kept bleeding long after the bat filled up and fluttered off.

Melody was still too young to care, but Sandy and I couldn't believe Terry's good luck.

"Wow, I wish I had a bat bite," Sandy said. "Terry gets all the good stuff."

Most of the Machiguengas had little scars from bat bites, but no one in our family had ever gotten one before, and having a scar from a bat bite was about the best badge of honor we could imagine. Besides, you wouldn't even feel it.

I must admit that as much as I wanted to get a bat scar, I kind of left it to chance until I could get bit by accident, as Terry had. Sandy, on the other hand, wasn't so patient. She slept for weeks with a corner of her net open and a little stalk of bananas inside. To our everlasting regret, neither of us ever got vampired. It would almost be worth a trip to Peru to try again.

On the other hand, I did get stung by isulas, which is almost as good as being bit by bats except that they don't leave a scar. People just have to take your word for it.

Isulas are big ants. Well ... "big ants" doesn't exactly do them justice — they're kind of like one-and-a-quarter-inch monster ants, the way they sting and all. We've seen Machiguenga men writhing on the floor after getting stung, and Machiguenga men don't writhe just to impress their girl friends.

I was the only one of us kids to get an isula bite, so I was kind of special even though my mom had already gotten stung once when she sat down in the outhouse. Since she might read this book, I'd better not say where she got stung, but you can assume it wasn't on the top of her head.

When I got stung, Terry and I were playing across the river on a rainy day. I was kind of scrabbling along a slippery bank and reaching into brushy places for handholds. All of a sudden I felt a scorching pain in my hand.

"Ayyyyoooouch!" I shouted, thinking in that split second that I'd been bitten by a snake. I jerked my hand back in time to shake off two isulas. Without even trying, I'd found a nest. The mad isulas swarmed and threatened and made little uuucchhyy noises with their pincers and we got out of there as if we thought they might chase us.

Terry paddled me home in the canoe, and by the time we raced up the bank to the house the pain had spread all through my hand and was headed up my arm. Running hadn't helped, since it speeded up the circulation. When you're eight years old and you know you're dying, you don't just sit down on the bank quietly to compose your final words.

Dad and Mom put mud on the stings and gave me a bunch of aspirins and I did my writhing in a hammock on the porch while the lymph nodes under my arm swelled up and I spiked a fever. Machiguengas who came by all got to hear the story, and they laughed to show how sympathetic they were.

Within eight hours or so the pain eased and I could brag about how cool it had been. Sandy wishes to this day that she could've been stung by an isula, but she never went over and stuck her fingers in the nest. No guts, no glory.

I also had the honor of having had rats chew on me. Right behind our house at Yarinacocha were two huge African palm trees that the rats loved to nest in.

Unfortunately, the rats had to go somewhere for food, and our house was handy.

When we had cats at home, the rats weren't such a problem. One cat in particular was a great ratter, and when she'd just had kittens she'd bring a rat in nearly every morning. Mom wasn't thrilled that she always left the bloody carcass under our coffee table, but hey, at least rats weren't tearing the place up at night.

When we didn't have cats, we had to be our own ratters, and I must say we had some really quality family time chasing rats in the middle of the night. It would start with Mom hearing a noise, creeping in her nightgown to the living room, and spotting the rodent.

"Hey, we've got a rat in the house," she'd hiss just loudly enough to wake some of us up. I think the rat wasn't supposed to hear her, but anything that would wake us up would certainly warn a rat.

Now what I'm about to say might sound a little barbarian, but you have to remember that the rats destroyed things and ate stuff and worst of all they chewed holes in Mom's Tupperware which was more terrible than the unpardonable sin.

And they never fell for the bait in our traps, so we had to be a bit more aggressive. Besides, they really did have the advantage, what with their speed and all.

"Where is he?" In seconds we tumbled downstairs armed with barbecue forks, hammers, long nosed pliers and other proven weapons. Mom usually hunted with a broom, presumably so she could sweep the rat in our direction, hocky-like. She would never have wanted to score with a rat, but she didn't mind an assist or two.

Once we had a general area to search, the hunt began. Mind you, I'm not talking about your typical hunt where you slowly sneak up on the game and whisper and carefully take aim. I'm talking about a slam bang, rip roaring, screaming and shouting chase that took all of us over tables, under couches, up and down stairs, behind curtains and through cabinets at full speed.

"Here he comes ... he's heading your way ... under the chair ... no, he turned around ... quick look under there ... wooooo ... WHAM ... missed him ... sweeeeep ... take the books off the shelf and see if you can get him with the pliers ..." Shouts of encouragement and despair ringing out in the night.

The worst of it was that whenever the rat got cornered, he'd head straight back for us and we'd have to jump out of the way and swing at him at the same time, which isn't as easy as it sounds. Trying to get out of the way of something you're trying to catch takes real coordination. For all of our bravado, we really didn't want to get too close until he was dead.

Well, occasionally we succeeded after up to an hour's chase, and we went back to bed knowing that our house was secure for one more night. Usually we tumbled back in bed just knowing that there was a tired, scared rat somewhere in the house.

In any case, our efforts didn't come even close to solving the problem, and I remember waking up some mornings with teeth marks in the calouses on my feet. Of course the calouses were so thick that it didn't hurt and didn't leave any scars and usually didn't even wake me up, so you'll just have to take my word for it. The fact that there wasn't any real evidence didn't keep me from bragging about it whenever we talked with our friends about how great our lives were.

The competition for best scars was pretty tough. One of our friends at Yarinacocha,

Heather Swanson, had the end of her toe bitten off by a piranha in the lake where we swam every day. The piranhas hardly ever bothered us, but Heather had a bit of blood on her toe and forgot to keep it moving.

"I'm gonna get revenge on that creep," vowed her brother Peter, who was addicted to fishing. True to his word he caught the fish and sure enough, his sister's toe was still in it. They put the toe in formaldehyde and took it to school for show and tell.

Another kid, Andy Lance, caught a big piranha and cut its head off right away. Then, just to feel how sharp its teeth were, he tapped on them with his finger. Quick as a wink, with a reflex action, the jaws snapped shut and bit a chunk out of his fingertip.

We had a tough time deciding which was better: getting your finger tip bitten off by a dead piranha or having part of your toe at school in a bottle of formaldehyde.

Terry was even lucky enough to get speared by a sting ray one summer. It happened on the first day of our vacation in Camisea and ruined his whole summer, since he couldn't go in the river to play with us. Boy did he have a dandy hole in his leg! He could stick a Q-Tip in almost a whole inch before it started healing shut. He still has a round purple scar there, sort of like an old bullet hole.

Sandy did come pretty close to having a great scar right on her face. As she remembers it, it was late afternoon and Terry and I were helping the men in Picha cut the airstrip with three-foot machetes. Mom sent Sandy to get us.

"It's supper time. Mom wants you to come home," Sandy called. Terry didn't hear her, so she walked up behind him about the time he changed position and swung his machete back. It cut her right across both lips. Mom was in despair.

"If only we had a doctor out here, he could stitch it up. Now she'll have a scar there for the rest of her life." Sandy could hardly believe her good luck.

Without a doctor, the best Dad could do was to put sulpha powder and a bandage on it and tell Sandy not to laugh or smile.

Now I can hardly believe this is true, but she swears that Terry and I tickled her to make her laugh, and that she had to laugh holding her cut lips together with one hand. For a long time she loved looking at her mouth in the mirror, but eventually it completely healed without a trace.

I didn't even get a good wound when a snake finally did bite me, and it was such a diddly thing I'd be embarrassed to write about it.

In the end, the only permanent scars I have are from carving balsa wood airplanes and boats. Everyone in the whole world tried to tell us how we should hold the knife just so, and cut by pushing it away from ourselves and use this thingy or that thingy to hold what we were carving and on and on. I don't know how we'd ever have gotten any scars that way. People who carve like that must not care what their friends think of them.

CHAPTER 12

Lonely Souls

"Dad, can we go with the teachers on the raft to Pucallpa this year?" It was a long-shot request from Terry and me, eleven and ten years old. We were in Camisea for three months of vacation from our school at Yarinacocha.

"Well, I'd say it's a possibility." A loophole-filled answer from Dad. From Mom, the answer would have been more straightforward. Like "No!" Or, "Over my dead body." It would be, after all, nearly 500 miles on a flooded river. That's why we'd asked Dad.

Peruvian schools were on a different schedule from our own, and got out for a long vacation starting in December. Every year the Machiguenga teachers took advantage of their time off to get more training at the Bilingual Education Center beside Yarinacocha.

Actually, in the early years of getting schools started in the jungle, the teachers had to come in for training so they could stay ahead of their students. They'd study first grade, then go out and teach it. As the students progressed, the teachers worked to keep one year ahead of them. Second graders teaching first graders. Third graders teaching second graders. And so on until all of the teachers could teach any grade.

Since teachers came from all over the jungle and SIL didn't have many airplanes, it wasn't easy to get everyone to the training school by plane. Living upriver from Pucallpa, the Machiguengas just floated down on huge rafts. We often saw those rafts drifting in to the waterfront and dreamed of the day we could ride on one.

As usual, Terry and Sandy and I flew back to Yarinacocha at the end of August to stay in the children's home while Dad and Mom and Melody moved over to Picha for a couple months. We envied them, but our parents thought we should get an education. Spoil sports. At any rate, we once again left the village waving bravely and swallowing the lumps in our throats while the airplane rocked us up on step and then off into the huge cumulus clouds.

While we lived in the children's home, played with our Yarina-based friends and went to school, the raft trip was never far from our minds. We nagged Dad about it regularly.

Every Saturday morning the kids staying in the children's home got to talk to their parents in the tribe on the two-way radios. Some kids were real talkative and a great joy to their parents. And, I might add, the envy of other parents who had kids like us.

"Hi, Sandy, how's school going? Over."

"Okay. Over."

"Have you been doing anything fun this week? Over."

"No. Over."

"What's been happening in school? Over."

"Nothing. Over."

It didn't help knowing that every other linguistic team in the jungle had their radios on and they were all tuned to the same frequency. Every stupid thing we said would be a topic of conversation at lunch tables in a dozen villages.

At least now we had the raft trip to talk about, and we kept asking if it was still on.

"Yup, we're planning on it, but they're going to build the raft over in Camisea so I won't know much about it until we get there in October. Mom and I want to make the trip your Christmas present this year."

"Great," we agreed, and couldn't wait until the next Saturday to hear more.

At the time, Dad was working hard on revising his translation of John and 1 Corinthians. He worked mostly with a man named Dionisio, who was one of Señor Pereira's boys. He was a real brain and eager to get the Bible in his own language. Dionisio had gone to a Bible school downriver for a few months and was a great preacher and Bible teacher, with a knack for making stories from the Bible come alive.

When Dionisio told the story of the Exodus from Egypt, you could just see the Egyptian chariots sinking in the mud on the bottom of the sea. Never mind that most Machiguengas didn't know what a chariot was. Or Egyptians either, for that matter.

Late in October a plane went out to move Mom and Melody from Picha back to Camisea. Dad would go by river in a canoe with an outboard motor. Thursday, October 26th, tragedy struck. We got a summary from Dad on the radio.

"We've got some really bad news, kiddies. Last week when I was coming down the Picha with Arturo and Dionisio, we had an accident and Dionisio drowned. We lost the motor and almost everything else we had out here." Dionisio's sisters and friends had been crying continuously. Our hearts sank.

"What about the raft trip?" It probably wasn't a very good time to ask, but we had to know.

"Well, I think you'd better not count on it this year. I thought we'd have the outboard to help steer the raft, but I don't think you boys should be on it if it's just drifting. It's too easy to run into something and get thrown off."

The canoe wreck was still vivid in Dad's mind. Although he couldn't get all of the details over the radio, we heard about it later. They had left Picha at noon on Thursday, loaded down with household equipment, including a table, chairs, pans, dishes, clothes and other supplies. Less than an hour later, as they splashed through a rapid, the propeller on the outboard hit a rock, breaking the shear pin. Dionisio, who was steering, panicked and swerved the canoe sideways into a huge tree that was lodged in the river with its branches sticking up above the water.

A wave threw Dad up into one of the branches and he pulled himself out of the strong current. Dionisio clung to a branch just down from him.

"*Totata*." Dad shouted for him to wait. Dad was trying to reach him when the current tore Dionisio's fingers loose and carried him downstream. He had never been very strong, didn't know how to swim, and was scared to death of water. He was certainly no match for the Picha's current. They never saw him again.

"............." There was lots of silence from our end of the radio as we digested the news. Dad's loss of a key translation helper and Bible teacher was certainly a lot sadder than our loss of a raft trip, but still....

Dad and Arturo had recovered a few things floating in the river. As they regrouped on a rocky beach, Arturo saw a tapir come to the surface right where Dionisio had gone under. Beyond a shadow of a doubt, Dionisio's soul had come back for others.

They spent the night drying out and shivering beside a campfire on the beach. Arturo shiverered at the thought of Dionisio's soul on the prowl, more dreadful than wild animals. Dad shivered in the cold.

The next morning someone came by in a canoe and took them to the mouth of the Picha, where there was a Catholic mission station. The priest was gracious and helpful, providing them with a boat and driver to get them to Camisea. Dad had just arrived before our radio sched.

It was a long, dejected week for Terry and me. We had had such high hopes. The next week there was even more bad news from Mom during the radio sched.

"Do you remember Akiraari?" We did. He was one of the sharper young men living in Camisea near us. He had started school late, so he already had a wife and a one-year-old son who sat and nursed while his mother and father learned to read and write.

"Well, the day after Dad got back Akiraari went out by himself to chop down a tree with a bee's nest in it. He wanted to get the honey. After the tree fell down he was trying to get the nest off and somehow his axe came down on his foot instead of the bees's nest. It went right through his foot between his big toe and the next one, about three inches back into his foot."

We were glued to the radio. Dionisio's soul had made it back to Camisea, where he originally came from, and deflected the axe. At least that's how the Machiguengas would explain such a strange accident exactly three days after the drowning.

"Akiraari tied his toes together with a vine and hobbled a long way back to his house and plonked down on the porch," Mom continued. "Blood was running out all over the place and we thought he'd pass out and die right then. It was such a mess that neither one of us wanted to fix it, but there wasn't anyone else who could do anything, so we cleaned it out and bandaged it and gave him some penicillin. Now all we can do is wait and see how he does. We told him to stay off it until it's better."

Sandy wished she'd been there to see it. We talked about how school was going and then passed the transmitter on to the next set of kids.

A week later the radio brought us the word we'd been hoping for. Dad had recovered a bit from his canoe wreck and was thinking optimistically again.

"Hey, boys, I think we just might be able to go on the raft after all, with some careful planning. Let's not give up on the idea yet. I've scheduled the plane to bring you out on December 17th." We were ecstatic. Neither we nor Dad knew what "careful planning" might mean, but I think it sounded good to Mom, who was waiting to fill us in on village news.

"Akiraari went fishing last week even though we told him not to, and then someone talked him into going tapir hunting. You know what that's like, getting into and out of the canoe and the river water and all. By the time he got back his foot was all split open and bleeding again. We kind of bawled him out, but he said if his family didn't have any meat, they couldn't eat, so what else could he do? We're just praying it doesn't get badly infected from the mud now."

All across the jungle the rainy season was starting. At Yarina we ate tree-ripened mangoes by the bushel, sloshed barefoot through the mud to and from school, and hoped for school cancellations because of the pounding rain. It rarely happened, but with metal roofs and screen windows on the classrooms, sometimes a thunderous downpour made it impossible to hear anything and blasting winds soaked everything within 12 feet of the windows. We could always hope.

As the water rose in the lake, more and more opportunities for fun opened up.

"Towner and Shonk went off the bank yesterday," someone announced at breakfast one day. That brave feat took a long, fast run and then a long jump, since you had to clear a bunch of debris on the shoreline to make it into the water. When the water was low it was impossible even for the best jumpers. One year Harry Price, who was older than us and had nerves of steel, jumped off the bank on his bicycle. He got kind of tangled up in the bicycle in mid air and he sort of landed on it. I never tried it.

"Is the water high enough to jump off Bigroot yet? Who's gonna be first off the arch?"

It was an annual question meant to test the bravery of every kid in our school. As soon as we were dismissed at noon we'd race to the children's home for lunch and then head to the lake for a quick swim before running back to school dripping wet. When school got out in the afternoon, we ran back to the lake. Although there were piranhas and alligators in the lake, they never bothered us much.

Bigroot was a huge banyon tree with several main trunks and hundreds of smaller ones. During high water, most of the trunks and trailing vines were in the water. Way at the top of the tree one thick branch made an arch, and jumping off the arch was a rite of passage. Being the first to jump off the arch each year was one of the ultimate signs of bravery, we thought.

People over thirty thought it was one of the ultimate signs of stupidity, since being the first one to jump meant plummeting twenty feet down through the middle of the tree into water that wasn't really deep enough. I had the honor one year and jammed my knees into my chin, but still came up with a huge smile on my face. There'd be time later to check for broken things in my body.

Rivers were rising out in the tribe as well. Saturday morning Dad updated us.

"The Indians have started cutting balsa logs for the raft. They're going to build it down at the mouth of the Camisea so they can launch it right into the Urubamba. How are things going in school? Over."

We passed on our news about activities at school and jumping off Bigroot so our parents would have something to worry about during the week. "Over."

People got so used to saying "over" at the end of each transmission on the radio that sometimes they accidentally said "over" instead of "amen" when they were done praying.

"Well, just to let you know, Akiraari is a pretty sick man. A couple days ago he came down with a bad fever and chills. He also started having spasms and got rigid all over. His back arched and his jaw tightened up and Dr. Eichenberger told us over the radio that he probably has tetanus. There isn't really anything we can do for him, but we've started him on massive doses of penicillin anyway. We're praying for him, because unless God works a miracle, Doc says Akiraari will probably die in a couple of days."

We had seen lots of Machiguengas die, but it sobered us to think of Akiraari all bent out of shape by repeated convulsions and spasms. We were pretty familiar with the threat of tetanus and were periodically forced to get the booster shots we hated. Listening to Dad over the radio, we were so glad we'd been shot.

Over the next three weeks, our raft took shape and Akiraari hovered between life and death. Dad and Mom alternated between hope and despair. Maybe God would heal him. Maybe not. Maybe this case was different. Maybe not. The Machiguengas poured hot water over him, bathed him with special herbal solutions and rubbed him with tobacco.

If any of Akiraari's family or neighbors inadvertently ate something that might magically make him sicker, they sent a woman to warm her hands over a hot coal and chant while she rubbed his leg.

He'd be better for a while, then worse. There were big open sores on his shoulder blades, head and buttocks from when his body spasmed on the woven mat he lay on. He was completely helpless, and demanded Dad and Mom's constant care to help cook for him, feed him and wash him. He didn't have any control over his bladder and bowels and always made a mess of himself. His suffering was horrible to watch, Dad and Mom said. Deep in his eyes there was wild fear.

A month after the accident, he seemed much better. He could move both arms and even hold something awkwardly in his hands.

"You're getting better, *Notomi*." He was my parents' Machiguenga "son." "By next week you should be sitting up." Encouraging words, hopefully prophetic. His raw body was beginning to relax somewhat.

Akiraari had frequently talked about wanting to believe in God. Venturo, a Machiguenga teacher and preacher, went over to pray with him on Saturday, but Akiraari said he couldn't talk that well yet.

That afternoon two terrible things

happened. First, a wild heron flew up to Akiraari's porch and landed on the very spot where he had plopped himself down when he first hobbled back from the accident.

Wild herons never came into the village. Without thinking, Akiraari's brother Atahualpa borrowed the teacher's shotgun and killed the heron, since the feathers are perfect for making arrows and the leg bones could be carved into flutes. After he plucked the heron, everyone could see that it had wounds in the very places where Akiraari had sores. It was a bad omen.

Then the final straw. As Akiraari lay suffering, he saw his spirit go up the pole of his house. That, he knew, was the end. The next morning he had a quick spasm and went into a coma before Dad and Mom could get there. He died at noon.

No one wanted to have anything to do with Akiraari's body. Not even his fifteen-year-old widow, who worried about her baby's life. Fear permeated the village. Everyone washed themselves with hot water and cut their hair. His widow drank a special potion to make her throw up, but it didn't work.

"I'll help take him downriver and bury

him," Dad offered, "but I can't get him to the canoe by myself. Someone will have to help me."

Atahualpa finally agreed to help. They wrapped the body in a mat and tied the ends shut. Then they carried it down to the canoe, traveled an hour downriver and buried it in a sandy bank above the Urubamba River.

All of Akiraari's family and neighbors went on a special diet: no fish with scales, no monkey, no watermelon or peanuts, no anything that might cause someone else to get sick.

In spite of all the precautions, Atahualpa paid for his foolishness in touching Akiraari's corpse. Exactly three days after he helped bury his brother, his wife gave birth in the jungle a little way from our house. Someone ran to get Mom.

"Camila just had her baby and she's sitting on it down by the trail. Can you help her?"

Mom hurried over to find that Camila was, indeed, squatting on the baby. It was still in its amniotic sack, blue from lack of oxygen, already dead. If only Atahualpa hadn't helped bury Akiraari.

Back in Yarinacocha, Terry and I were

getting ready for our trip. We gathered equipment, bought new flashlights and fresh batteries, and kept up our running radio dialogue with Dad. The raft was taking shape and now had a small floor and a thatched roof on it. We'd be flying out in about a week. Our excitement infected the whole children's home.

Back in Camisea Camila buried her dead baby and cut her own hair. Under the circumstances, she should have known to be very careful for a while. She certainly should have known to not to talk to any other women who hadn't had a child die yet, and especially not to look at their babies for a few days.

Still, when Adela came to get medicine for her baby, who had a severe case of thrush, Camila was careless. She greeted Adela and then walked right up to her, pulled back the cloth over the baby's face and looked at it. The baby died exactly three days after Camila's baby.

Sunday morning Terry and I finally boarded a little float plane and said goodbye to Sandy, who was crying on the bank as we taxied away from shore. Two hours later we landed on the chocolate brown Camisea and jumped onto the muddy river bank. Melody hugged and kissed us like long lost brothers. Tiahuaca, our dog, jumped up and down all over us until we were scratched and covered with mud. It was great to be home, but it was a somber home. Everyone was talking about Dionisio, and Akiraari, and Camila and Adela's babies.

"See," they soberly reminded each other, "the souls of the dead never want to go alone. The third day after they die, you have to be really careful or they'll get you."

Even those who genuinely wanted to believe in the power of God over spirits and souls were shaken by the graphic reality of their recent experiences.

The next morning, somewhat subdued, we waved Mom and Melody off in the plane, then made final preparations for our trip.

CHAPTER 13

Riding the Flood

When Dad had told us we could go on the raft trip, he knew the river would be high, but he didn't reckon on the Urubamba being at its peak. Heavy rains Monday afternoon brought logs and debris swirling past on foaming brown currents. The awesome power of so much rushing water gave me chills. Fortunately, now that the plane had left to take Mom and Melody back to Yarinacocha, it was too late for Dad to change his mind. This was going to be a great ride.

Early Tuesday we heard Dad's familiar wake-up call, meant only for us but loud enough to rouse everyone in the village. Not that any Machiguengas would be asleep after 5:00.

"Ronny, Get up. Terry, Get up," he shouted. "I've got some fried eggs and oatmeal for you. Let's get it down and get going."

As quickly as we could, we wolfed down big servings, grabbed our little bags of essentials and canoed down to the mouth of the Camisea in the damp fog. The Machiguengas had already loaded their baggage and animals on the raft and were eager to get started.

We huddled on the muddy bank for prayer. Then Arturo untied the thick vine that held the raft to a tree stump and we were carried off to our fates.

Within seconds we floated out of the Camisea's mouth and into the much bigger

Urubamba. Whirlpools, undertows and backwaters spun and jolted us. Uprooted trees, unmanned, banged into us. Four men manned the oars, working to keep us pointed with the current. In dangerous spots, the goal was always to have the logs going parallel with the current rather than sideways. Of course in dangerous spots we usually didn't have much influence on how the logs were pointed, and we just hung on for dear life.

Our raft was about 30 feet long and 12 feet wide, made of twelve big balsa logs that were pointed on the ends. Hardwood poles were pinned across the logs to hold them together, and for good measure everything was lashed with vines and the strong inner bark of the balsa trees.

About 16" above the logs was a pona floor that covered the middle 2/3 of the raft. Over the floored section we had a low thatched roof to protect us from torrential rainstorms and merciless sun. The roof came right down to the floor so we didn't need walls. All in all, it was a cozy home for the nine of us.

The only way to control the raft was with two huge oars fastened to "Y" sticks braced on each side at the front. The paddles on the ends of the sticks were two-foot circles and stuck out like ears. If we wanted to do some serious paddling, it took two men on each paddle.

We didn't really have that much control over the raft even with the oars. It weighed a couple tons and pretty much went wherever the current dragged it. Still, a little control was better than none.

We had all of the comforts of home. There was plenty of water for bathing and drinking, though it was dirty brown and there were lots of things floating in it besides us. Our toilet was the poop deck at the back of the raft. It flushed automatically, if you know what I mean. There was a coop by the poop, filled with squawking, crowing, flapping, clucking chickens and ducks that didn't want to be there. Two parrots with their wings clipped sat on the roof and *rrraaawwwkkked* our passage.

Stashed on the floor were woven baskets of coffee beans and barrels of corn to sell downriver, plus cooking pots, manioc, stalks of bananas, bedding and clothes. If we were lucky, all of this would stay on the raft and keep dry. No one is ever that lucky.

Since it would be impossible to paddle our raft to shore every time we needed something, or to chase animals in it, we towed a dugout canoe alongside. We could use it for errands, or we could all climb aboard and abandon the raft in an emergency. Never mind that the canoe tipped over easier than the raft, and that it already had three steel barrels of corn in it.

Those first few hours were an adrenaline rush. Never had we gone so fast on the Urubamba without a motor.

"How do you like it?" Dad asked. He was as excited as we were.

"This is *neat*," I exclaimed. "I could do this for the rest of my life." Terry and I were bouncing back and forth between the front and back, making general nuisances of ourselves as we all raced along between towering trees. All of the familiar gravel bars were underwater and we flew right over the tops of them. When we went through rapids, the high waves splashed up through the logs and sloshed against our legs.

Late in the morning we headed into a particularly wavy rapid. Water swirled around us, waves washed over the raft and the current spun us around, dangerously close to the bank. The combination of waves and cross currents swamped the canoe, which overturned, dumped the three barrels of corn and banged into the raft.

"Cut the canoe loose," Arturo yelled at Megiri. Megiri was just a boy like me and even more afraid than I was. He wasn't about to let go of his hand hold. While he hesitated and before anyone could cut the rope holding the canoe to the raft, it swung around like a battering ram and banged into the chicken coop, setting ducks and chickens free. Now we had ducks, chickens and three barrels of corn all trying to get away, and our chase canoe was full of water. The ducks were delighted. The chickens were mad as wet hens.

As soon as we had survived the rapid, we sloshed the water out of the canoe and two Machiguengas took off after the ducks and corn. The chickens, of course, had nowhere to go so catching them was a pretty fun game of crawling under the floor, up on the roof and round and round the raft.

"Here he comes. Grab him when he comes out from under the floor." Or, "She's out on the oar. Swim out there and grab her." Flapping feathers exploded around us, but sooner or later we got them all.

The ducks, on the other hand, had a pretty clear advantage over the canoe.

Three of them made a complete getaway, ducking underwater with big smiles on their beaks whenever the canoe got close and popping back up to the surface far beyond reach. And we only got two of the three barrels of corn back, a terrible $4.00 loss.

"Did you see Megiri. He was as scared as a woman. He just sat there holding on like a sick little old man." Now that the crisis had passed, it was time to laugh and make jokes about the whole thing. And to think about how hungry we were.

"What have we got for lunch?" Terry asked. Chasing chickens had worked up our appetites.

"Lunch? We don't have any lunch," Dad answered as if we should have known that you don't eat lunch on a raft. "Have a couple of bananas to hold you over until supper." We were glad for our big breakfast, but it did seem like quite a while since we'd eaten.

We had planned on passing the mouth of the Picha River the next day, but with our hyper speed we closed in on it about 2:00 in the afternoon. That section of river included the famous Carpintero Rapids, where water churned over boulders that sat in the middle of the river. On the left side was a ragged cliff of red shale, constantly being eroded by the tons of water that crashed into it hour after hour. I had heard of the Carpintero ever since I could remember. Bad in low water, it would be worse now.

The whole river was boiling like hot chocolate. Up ahead we saw high waves tossing foam and debris into the air. Most of the river funneled directly into a huge rock, and wherever most of the river went, most of us were likely to follow. It would have been a perfect place to get into the canoe and paddle our way out of trouble, but we were caught off guard.

The four men at the paddles laughed and joked. A really bad sign. When Machi men get slap happy, you can assume they think they have just minutes left to live. Their muscles bulged as they strained to pull us out of the main current.

"Put yourself into it. Harder now. We're going to hit the rock and die." Har har har. "Stronger, you weakling. You're pulling like a little girl." Louder laughter and falsetto "aiiieeeeees." At the last minute they gave up and grabbed onto anything they could. We remained very much in the main current.

With a roar and a splash we went under.

Water covered the logs and soaked the floor. Two hundred yards of wide-eyed, white-knuckled anticipation, then a loud splintering crash as we hit the rock. The left paddle snapped off like a twig and the raft lurched, then crunched along the cliff, still mostly in one piece.

The baptized chickens weren't pleased. The parrots on top, unaware of how close they had come to being fish food, squawked happily in the wind and said Machiguenga words that I can't repeat.

With only one oar all we could do was spin the raft around in circles, completely at the river's mercy. It was clearly a time for desperate measures. The Machis were talking fast.

Suddenly, with a death-defying leap, Arturo sailed for the bank, holding the heavy vine tied to the front of the raft. He landed in waist deep water, scrambled through the mud, whipped the vine around the nearest tree like a saddle horn and hung on with all his might as he waited to see if the vine would hold and stop the raft. No bull wrestler could have done it better. Especially in a river.

We hit the end of the vine with a jerk that nearly pulled it out of Arturo's hands, but the tree, the vine and the piece of raft it was tied to all held. With a bump, the raft banged into the bank and stopped. Within seconds we were safely tethered and scrambling out to assess the damages.

The only significant loss was the broken paddle. Although we'd have to replace it, at least we didn't have to fix the whole raft. Unfortunately our tool kit didn't include an axe to chop down a tree.

"Go back to the mission and get an axe," Arturo suggested. "We'll get started while we're waiting."

Three of the Indians walked back through the jungle to the mouth of the Picha, where the same priest who had helped Dad and Arturo after Dionisio's accident loaned them his axe. In the meantime, the remaining Machiguengas started to work with machetes while Terry and I made little streams in the sand.

Within three hours the amazing Indians had chopped down a tree, cut out a section of it and split the section into boards. While someone returned the axe to the mission, those who stayed behind used their machetes to cut the boards into rough circles with stems to tie them onto their long shafts. Just to be on the safe side, they made two new paddles so we'd have a spare.

By 5:00 we were more or less back in business, so we floated for another half hour before tying up at a semi-protected section of sand bar for the night. Close by were some Machiguengas' gardens where we could find fruit and manioc.

Mario and I made a fire. Terry and the others collected firewood and food. By dark we were eating a fabulous supper of roasted fish, boiled cooking bananas, coffee and taffy. Dad wasn't quite as impressed with it as we were.

"I kind of prefer steak and potatoes with all the trimmings," he said as we raved over the fish. We were glad our taste buds hadn't been ruined by life outside the jungle.

That night Dad and Terry and I slept on the raft in luxury, listening to the waves slap the balsa logs. The Indians preferred to sleep on the beach. They lay beside the fire on big, soft balsa leaves, secure in the knowledge that the sandbar wouldn't come untied and drift off in the night. The raft, on the other hand, might.

Ringing machetes woke us up at 5:00 a.m. The Indians were already boiling bananas and manioc for breakfast while someone refined the new paddles. At 5:30, fed and loaded, we floated off into the mist.

Before we even saw it, we heard it — the raging roar of another bad spot. It was nearly the reverse of the Carpintero, with all of the river charging full blast into the right hand bank. Water mounded up against the bank and then swirled off into whirlpools and undertows. This looked even worse than the Carpintero, and we had to buy some time. Getting the raft stopped would be nearly impossible, since it was picking up speed as we headed downhill.

"This is too dangerous. We've got to get tied up to the bank. Grab the vine."

"We can't stop the raft. It's going too fast."

"If we don't stop it we'll all die." Machiguengas lived with death all around them and talked about it a lot more casually than we liked.

Too fast or not, several of them jumped off the raft and held fast until the raft swung to a stop beside the bank.

"Get in the canoe with Megiri and Andres," Arturo instructed us. "They can paddle you past the worst spots. We'll take the raft through and meet you downriver."

"Aww, do we have to," I pled with Dad. We didn't want to miss any of the action.

"Yeah, we need to do what they tell us on this one. They're afraid the undertow is going to pull the raft into the worst spot, and they want it to be as light as possible. Besides, they don't want to be responsible for us while they're trying to get the raft through. We'd just be in the way."

We climbed in the canoe to watch. Once set free, the raft quickly gained speed. Four men pumped at the oars hoping to outwit the treacherous undertow and miss the worst of it.

"Do you think they'll make it, Dad?" To me, it didn't look likely. The raft was barely responding to all the hard work. I could just picture the raft shattering on impact, dumping all its passengers into the swirling water and leaving us all stranded.

"Oh yeah, they know what they're doing." Dad had a lot of confidence in the Machiguengas, but he didn't sound as sure as he might have. Just a month before, he had watched one drown.

From our front row seats we could see the whole show. The men heaved on the oars. The raft rose and fell on the building waves, heading full speed for the high bank. In seconds it would all be over. I wasn't breathing.

A few feet were all it took to clear the bank. The raft leaned precariously against the mound of water and went under for its second baptism, but rushed uncrunched away from the cliff, both oars still intact. We inhaled and cheered and paddled off to catch up.

Later in the day we picked up some Piro Indians who were hitch hiking on a sand bar. They wanted a lift to Bufeo Poso, they said, but got off sooner at the Piro Bible School. The Piros already had quite a lot of the Bible translated into their language.

That night we stayed with the German missionaries who ran the Bible school. They fed us venison and boiled manioc and invited us to sleep on the dirt floor of their school house. The Machiguengas opted for the raft, which was tied in a rather swift spot. If we lost the raft during the night, at least they would be aboard.

Our third morning started at 4:45. As we cruised along at midmorning, one of the ducks escaped from the coop. Quick as a wink Andres jumped into the canoe and went after it, paddling within a hand grab. Just as he shot out his hand, the duck ducked and we all burst out laughing. Startled and embarrassed, Andres laughed harder than all of us. The race was on.

The duck surfaced just upriver from us and hurtled past the raft, flapping and paddling like a waterwheel. Andres was right behind it in the canoe, and as the canoe tore past the raft Mario jumped in. They closed in on the duck and Mario reached to grab it. Too late. The duck went down and we all roared, waiting to see where it would come up next. Since it stayed close to the raft, everyone joined in, grabbing sticks to try and hit it when it came up.

After ten minutes of fun, someone hit the breathless thing too hard and injured it's leg. It gave up and started drowning. Andres and Mario closed in and grabbed it before it disappeared, then threw it back into the coop.

A couple of hours after the duck chase we approached Sepa, an isolated jungle prison colony for murderers and dangerous political prisoners. We had to check in with the police there, but it took forever to get to shore. A long series of whirlpools took us in big circles, down, up, across and back down the river. For an hour we were within sight of the town but going nowhere.

When we finally pulled in to shore, we

went directly to see the new director of the colony. At the time, we never imagined that in a year Terry and I would help chase down four of his escaped murderers. But that's another story.

We explained who we were and then sold him one of the parrots, a bag of coffee beans, and several of the chickens and ducks. To celebrate our lightened load and successful sale, the Machis plucked the injured duck, laughing and enjoying its pain. They loved to torture animals, so they often plucked chickens and ducks before killing them. I tried not to look, or listen, but it was kind of hard in such close quarters. When they were through, it made great soup.

By the time we settled in for our third night, we could see flashes of lightning upriver, and hear pounding thunder in the distance. The Machiguenga villages were getting another good soaking. That would mean an even higher river soon.

Once again the Indians slept on the beach. Dad and Terry and I got the floor of the raft to ourselves and were soundly sleeping when the river rose so high that it pulled the raft loose. Fortunately, the Indians seldom all slept at the same time, especially since they'd been keeping a wary eye on the water level.

"Father, the raft is loose," someone called out around midnight. Dad was "Father" to most of the teachers on the trip. I'm not sure what they expected him to do about it.

We bolted awake in time to see dark shapes jumping aboard as the raft slowly pulled away from the flooding beach. The water had already risen a couple of feet and had not crested yet.

Heavy black clouds covered the night sky. It was so dark that we couldn't tell where the river ended and the trees began, nor where the trees ended and the sky began. It was hard to see each other, much less obstacles in the river. For the first and only time the whole trip, even Dad was afraid. The roaring of rapids filled our ears, but it was impossible to tell which way to go through them.

Our puny flashlights probed the night, but only warned us of what was coming. By the time we could see anything, there was no way to avoid it. We banged into the bank and trees. We bobbed up and down on the waves, and felt water sloshing around us and our stuff. Every once in a while we sped past the light of a campfire on shore, then back into total darkness. No one slept, in case we suddenly had to swim for our lives. Our flashlights grew dimmer as the batteries wore down.

By the time we could distinguish between trees and sky and river, we were all exhausted from the strain, but we were alive and still afloat. There would be plenty of time later for naps, piled one on top of the other.

That night was our last one tied up to the shore. Once the Urubamba and Tambo Rivers joined to make the Ucayali River, the rapids petered out and we could drift 24 hours a day.

The Ucayali was wide and full of drifting trees. Those trees, in fact, gave us some great fun.

"Hey, let's go climb on that one," I suggested, pointing to a particularly big one. Terry wasn't interested, but Megiri and I paddled the canoe over to a massive trunk that floated fifty yards away. We climbed aboard and explored the branches and roots, all still intact. In fact, it's the only time I've ever climbed a tree floating down the river. That was more fun than a wild pig stampede.

"Let's build a fire and roast some bananas, Megiri." I was thinking about moving in permanently. We broke off some of the smaller twigs, pulled some matches out of a pocket and got a pretty good blaze going on a dry spot. It was sort of like sawing off the branch you're sitting on, but this log could burn for a long, long time before we sank it. Megiri went back to the raft for bananas and we had a mighty fine lunch, just coasting down the river on our private tree house.

Things turned routine for the last three days. We pretty much stayed on the raft because the river was so high we seldom saw any land to get out on. Once in a while we'd paddle the canoe into a town and stock up on basic supplies like candy and sugar, then hurry to catch up with the raft again. Terry and I took turns at the oars, not doing anything significant but still feeling as if we were helping somehow.

The farther downriver we got, the more pink river dolphins we saw. They played around the raft, sometimes four or five of them jumping and blowing in a row. Along with more dolphins, there was more river traffic. We often waved at dugouts, motor launches, and other rafts that shared our flowing highway.

We arrived at Pucallpa tired and wet

after dark on Christmas day, seven days after leaving Camisea. Since no one was expecting us, we spent the night swatting mosquitoes on the raft. Mary and Joseph in a liquid Bethlehem. In the morning we shocked everyone by showing up at Yarinachocha in the back of a chartered truck. Since the trip normally took 10-15 days, our seven-day race must have set some kind of a record.

Sadly, this adventure had a bit of an unhappy ending. Because we'd had so much fun, and because all the kids at Yarinacocha were jealous, our teachers made us write down the story of our trip. That's how I know that everything you've just read is true, even though it's not exactly how my dad remembers it. My mom has repressed the whole thing.

CHAPTER 14

The Posse

One clear summer morning we sat at
the breakfast table in Camisea eating
oatmeal with powdered milk on it and coffee
cake with powdered charcoal on it. I'd been
inspired when I woke up, and baked the
coffee cake in a frying pan on our cook fire
all by myself. We were eating it anyway. It
was toasty black on top and runny white in

the middle, like a lot of the cakes I baked.

From our breakfast table we had a beautiful view across the Urubamba River, and this morning, while we crunched coffee cake and swallowed whole globs of sticky hot oatmeal, we suddenly saw several Indians running toward our house and jabbering excitedly about something on the far bank. We went to see what was happening.

"See those men over there?" Miguel pointed with his lips.

Four men were indeed walking along the rock bar across the river. They were all dressed in shirts, pants and shoes, obviously outsiders.

Having four outsiders walk past the village was akin to discovering snow on the front porch. It just didn't happen in Camisea. After all, the closest place to walk *from* downriver was a long, long ways away, through dense jungle. The closest place to walk *to* upriver was even farther, and they would have to climb over a high, jungle covered cliff on their way.

"Who *are* those guys?" Sandy wanted to know, as if we could read their name tags from 100 yards away. Dad was thinking hard, but he didn't say anything right off.

The mystery of it all wasn't lost on our Machiguenga neighbors, who stared and whispered suspiciously to each other. Telegraphically, the word spread that four strangers were on the far shore, heading upriver without a canoe and not even calling to greet us. They carried almost nothing with them, and hurried past as quickly as they could.

As the men disappeared back into the jungle upriver, the Indians drifted to our house. Excited speculation ran rampant and rumors came to life like so many turtles hatching out of their eggs. Finally Dad broke in.

"Several days ago on the radio they said that four convicts had escaped from Sepa, heading upriver. I wonder if that's them." Silence washed over the front porch briefly, and then chattering erupted once again.

Sepa was the prison colony seventy or eighty miles downriver, reserved for some of Peru's worst criminals. Murderers and dangerous political prisoners were about the only types that were sent there. It was a jungle version of Alcatraz, built on the assumption that even if someone escaped, they'd have nowhere to go. We'd been there several times to report our activities to the police as we traveled here and there.

The Machis wondered back and forth how anyone could have made it this far without food. They themselves wouldn't have considered such a dangerous trip.

We found out later that these particular prisoners had behaved themselves well enough to earn some freedoms. Rather than being chained together as they worked in the gardens around the colony, they had been free to move about at will. When the right opportunity came, they just walked off the job and disappeared into the jungle. No one thought they'd get far. Certainly not as far as Camisea.

Well, that should have been the end of it. Anyone other than my dad would have reported it to the authorities and left it at that. The men would die of snake bite or jaguar attacks or the police would come get them and we would hear about it on our two-way radio after it was all over.

My dad, on the other hand, saw a super opportunity for the Machiguengas to gain some self confidence in their relations to outsiders. After all, the Machiguengas traditionally ran off into the jungle whenever they were threatened, but with more and more outsiders coming in, there were less places to run to.

What better way to boost self esteem than to go capture four hardened criminals from Sepa? Just to be sure everyone possible gained self confidence, he said Terry and I could go along. Since he himself already had plenty, acquired while helping to win World War II, he opted to stay home.

The rag tag posse that we formed would have made most criminals laugh outright. Fortunately, these particular convicts didn't know that they could scatter us in an instant by making faces and saying "Boo!" The Machiguengas genuinely feared outsiders. On the other hand, we did outnumber them three to one. Every man in the village, it seemed, needed more self confidence.

We ranged considerably in experience and confidence. At the top of the heap was Julio, an abnormally tall, bearded man whose father wasn't a Machiguenga. He had served in the military and spoke some Spanish and looked more like a criminal than the criminals. He was probably the only one of us who didn't need a better self image.

At the bottom of the heap was — well — the rest of us. The bottom of the heap was quite a lot larger than the top. Venancio was an adopted slave who only had one good eye and one good button on his shirt. He looked at the world with his head cocked to one side and his belly sticking out. Chonki wore his traditional cushma and his headband with the bird feather bangs. Both his eyes were good, but you couldn't see them.

Justo was a kid like Terry and me. His bow and arrow were real weapons, but he would never have used them on anyone. He never dreamed that outsiders were more afraid of bows and arrows than of guns.

Miguel, our village headman, had feather bangs and face paint like Chonki, but he wore a shirt and pants and carried a shotgun. I have no idea if he had any ammunition for it. All in all we had four shotguns, Dad's .22 rifle and the bow and arrows. Of course there wasn't a single pair of shoes in the whole posse.

Dad gave us a quick briefing before he sent us off. Phrases like "may be armed" and "very dangerous" and "be careful" and "don't let them grab your guns," if I remember correctly. He probably even told the Machis not to give the convicts our guns if they asked for them. Machiguengas are very accomodating people.

Terry got to carry our rifle. I was jealous, not because I wanted the burden of carrying it, nor because I had any thought of using it, but because I knew that whoever carried it would get to hold it for the pictures afterward.

We overloaded a couple of canoes that sank to the gunwhales and crossed the Urubamba, bailing furiously. It was a sparkling day and the whole atmosphere couldn't have been more like a family picnic at the beach. The whole posse was laughing and making jokes. In other words, they were frightened.

Of course once we picked up the strangers' trail everyone got quiet. The Indians wouldn't have much of an idea what to do when we caught up with the convicts, but at least they were expert hunters.

It wasn't a difficult trail to follow, since our prey all had shoes and left plenty of signs of their passing. Where they could, they walked on the sand or rock beaches, only going into the jungle when they had to. We saw where they swiped some bananas and papayas as they walked through a garden. They had walked steadily since we first saw them and were a good ways ahead of us, but the Machis moved quickly over rocks and through the jungle, Julio in the lead. Terry and I scrambled to keep up.

Somehow Julio knew when we were getting close. All 12 of us got quieter and stealthier, hoping to surprise them. Whenever the footprints broke out of the jungle onto a beach, we still crept behind bushes and trees, out of sight.

"Neri, pineakeri." Julio caught his first glimpse of them and invited us all to look. "Keep your heads down," he whispered to Terry and me. Our blonde hair waved like white flags in the wind. He was afraid one of the men had already seen Terry.

We worked our way back into the jungle. When we broke out onto the next gravel bar, we'd be right on top of them. Apprehension filled the quiet posse. We couldn't see very far ahead of us through the thick trees. If they had seen us, they might be waiting in ambush, the element of surprise on their side instead of ours. I worked to keep as quiet as possible, and to stay between two men with guns. No one said anything. Fortunately, no one said "Boo."

Suddenly Julio broke out of the jungle and we ran after him. The four men were in the open, sitting ducks. Sitting, as a matter of fact, around a little fire while they peeled bananas to boil. It was about as dramatic and tense as a nap.

This was all rather unexpected. Having gotten psyched up for a glorious victorious capture, no one quite knew what to do with four ordinary men sitting down to lunch. The posse, suddenly bashful and embarrassed by their bristling guns, deteriorated into jokes and laughter. Only Julio kept his head and started asking them questions.

"Where are you going?" The most basic of questions first, in Spanish.

"We're on our way to Quillabamba. Last night our canoe drifted away with all of our stuff in it." Some of the Machis, at least those who understood a bit of Spanish, nodded their heads sympathetically. I could just picture them thinking that maybe we could loan them another canoe.

"Where did you come from?" Julio persisted.

"Atalaya." It was the wrong thing to say. The Machiguengas knew that no outsiders in their right minds would attempt to canoe from Atalaya to Quillabamba. It would take weeks, and just getting through the Pongo above Timpia would be all but impossible. Murmers rippled through the posse.

"We're taking you back to Camisea," Julio finally told them. For emphasis, he pulled the trigger on his shotgun and blasted a shot into the air. Everyone, especially the posse, jumped.

I have absolutely no idea what we would have done if those men had decided they would just stay seated around the fire. Passive resistance would have completely immobilized us.

Fortunately for Machiguenga self esteem then and ever after, the convicts took Julio's gun and the rest of the posse seriously. Outsiders were deathly afraid of Indians, and especially Indians with bows and arrows and face paint. The weakest members of our posse became our greatest strength.

Trembling, the escapees stood up, collected their cooking pot and meager food, and dejectedly started back downriver. They looked hungry and ragged and exhausted. Terry, eager to show that he was as serious as Julio, zinged a bullet into the trees. Since it didn't make as much noise as the shotgun had, it wasn't quite as shocking, but the message was hopefully clear: "We're a lot more dangerous than we look, so don't get any ideas."

It was quite hard to feel like a hero when the men were so cooperative. I think Dad's great lesson would have been far more effective if we'd had to truss the men up and carry them pig-like on poles back downriver. Still and all, when we eventually crossed back over to Camisea, the bank was lined with impressed onlookers. The whole posse stood straight and tall. Well — at least straight. None of them were particularly tall.

Of course we took pictures, posed like triumphant hunters on safari. There were just two problems with the pictures. The first is that with just a couple of exceptions it's very difficult to tell which ones are the posse and which are the prisoners. They all look rather rumpled and dejected. The second is that Dad thought it wouldn't be good to have Terry and me in the picture, since we shouldn't have been out helping recapture murderers. So after Terry went to all that trouble of lugging the .22 there and back, Abram held it in the picture.

Dad radioed Sepa to let the police know that we had their escapees in custody, and the four prisoners were fed hearty meals and put under house arrest in the village. They begged Dad to let them go, but he was unrelenting. Just to be sure they didn't run away again, Julio took their shoes. They wouldn't think of charging off into the jungle barefoot with their tender feet.

That worked for a while, but as I said, the Machiguengas are very accommodating. Toward evening one of the prisoners called out to the school teacher, who understood a good bit of Spanish.

"Would it be possible to get our shoes back so we can go to the bathroom? We can't walk into the jungle barefoot."

"Of course. Wait a minute and I'll get them." The teacher was quick to oblige.

By morning our prisoners, the pride of the posse, were long gone. This was a bit embarrassing to Dad, since a police boat was on its way upriver to fetch them, but the Machiguengas took it in stride. They'd catch them again, they figured, sort of like the cat that enjoys letting the mouse get away so he can catch it again. Two ego-boosting lessons with just one set of prisoners. Such a deal.

With the police boat on its way, the second posse had a smaller objective. They would simply track the men down and force them to wait by the river. Although we begged, Terry and I didn't get to go along for the same reason we didn't get to be in the picture. The police from Sepa might not approve.

When we heard what happened, I was glad I wasn't along after all.

It was easy work tracking the men down. They hadn't gotten very far because for quite a ways there were no beaches on our side of the river. They'd had to work their way through the jungle.

Once the Machis caught up with the two-time escapees, they quickly got them to go down by the river. Everyone sat down at the base of a high bank, and that's where they were when the police boat caught up with them.

At the same instant the boat touched the bank, two policemen jumped for shore with guns in their hands. As soon as they were within range, they swung the guns like massive billy clubs, whacking the criminals on the muscles of their arms and legs with bone-cracking force. The men screamed and toppled to the ground, where they were completely immobilized before being thrown groaning into the boat.

It was a very sober posse that arrived back at Camisea. Now they had seen firsthand how to deal with outsiders. It was a lesson they didn't learn, and our appreciation for the gentle Machiguengas rose one more notch.

CHAPTER 15

Yarinacocha to Tingo Maria

"Kids," Dad announced one day at lunch in Yarinacocha, "we've just gotten an answer to our prayers." We immediately all set about trying to determine which prayers he was talking about.

There were the ongoing prayers for personal growth. And the ones about Machiguengas with special struggles. And the one about an inexpensive way to get to Lima.

"Oh no — it's not some cheap way to get to Lima, is it?" Sandy asked.

"They want us to take the Chevy carryall to Lima so it can be sold. They'll pay all the expenses. I told them we'd be glad to." Our hearts sank at yet another special provision.

"But that car always breaks down and it smells funny. How will we ever make it all the way to Lima?" Terry blurted out, forgetting that this was an answer to prayer.

Terry was 12, I was 11, Sandy 8 and Melody 5. We were all old enough to know that this answer to our prayers was a bad deal. Any car in the jungle was a bad deal, and this one had been there three years. Just getting it over the road from Lima to the jungle had taken ten years off its useful life. Keeping it there three years had taken off another ten.

Now that the carryall was decrepit and constantly breaking down light years away from the auto parts stores that it was addicted to, it was time to sell it. No one was quite sure if the green exterior was paint or mildew. The green interior was definitely mildew.

There weren't many people who could take it to Lima. Of those who could, none would. The road was horrible. The thin air at the 16,500 foot pass would kill off the car and everyone in it. Landslides and broken down trucks would block the road. Only my dad thought all this sounded like a great way to save money.

One of the problems with my family was that we could never turn down the opportunity to save money on a trip. Now that simple philosophy would get us our first trip across the Andes and nearly cost us our lives.

It was time for our second furlough, and although Dad and Mom were excited, the rest of us didn't look forward to it any more than we had our first furlough. Life in America was so foreign compared to our jungle home.

Still, our parents could hardly leave us with the Indians for a year, so they dragged us with them, figuratively kicking and screaming. Reminders of special treats like

Dunkin' Donuts and TV shows like Hogan's Heroes, McHale's Navy and Gilligan's Island failed to raise our enthusiasm.

Packing for furlough was never fun, and was certainly never a good way to begin a period of rest and relaxation. By the time we had ensured that stuff left behind wouldn't be eaten by termites, chewed by rats, rotted by mildew, or rusted through from the oppressive humidity, we were all pretty tired and the Chevy carryall was pretty full. Full to the ceiling, in fact.

"Are you sure it's going to clear the rocks," a skeptical neighbor asked just before our departure. Designed for smooth U.S. highways, the glorified station wagon sagged rather badly, its underside precariously close to things that stuck up in the road. On our road, anything that wasn't a hole was sticking up.

"Oh yeah," we heard Dad answer with whole-hearted optimism. In spite of all evidence to the contrary, Dad still thought everything would turn out okay.

All six of us plastered happy smiles over our tired and crabby faces as we pulled away from our jungle home. As usual with life threatening departures, many colleagues and friends were there to see us off.

"God bless you!"

"We'll be praying for you!"

"Have a good trip!"

"God go with you!" Of course they were all glad they weren't going with us, and probably immediately turned around and raised their hands to heaven thanking God that they weren't in the car. We were all pretty sure we'd never see each other again, but no one said so.

Three of us sat in the front. That would have been Dad and Mom and whoever was in most immediate danger of either throwing up or getting thrown out a back window for being a pain. The other three had the back seat as we sped off at ten miles an hour on the only road connecting Pucallpa to Lima.

"It stinks in here," we unanimously complained within minutes. "Can we open the windows?"

"If we open the windows, the car will fill with dust," Mom reasoned. "We'll be filthy." The road was either slippery mud or choking dust. This being the beginning of the dry season, it was pure dust.

"If we don't open the windows, we'll be dead," argued Sandy without much exaggeration. So we drove with the windows all wide open to cut down on the heat, humidity, mildew spores and engine fumes. Dust clouds boiled into the car and coated us from head to toe.

Within six hours, every hair on our heads and in our noses was dusty white and starch stiff. Now and then we'd pat the seats and raise little white puffs of dust just for a diversion. When we clambered out of the car for rest breaks, we looked like a host of ghosts.

Driving this road required frequent rest breaks. It was made of rocks and crushed gravel, though that makes it sound smoother than it was. In a desperate fight to save the road from tropical downpours, the rocks had been hauled from the Aguaytia River and packed into the ever shifting red clay. Driving on the boulders was about as pleasant as sitting on a jack hammer.

Everything in the car including our teeth and eyeballs rattled and banged. Things under the car — probably including a few important things like the oil pan and the steering linkage — scraped and crunched. The only thing fun about this part of the trip was that we were going somewhere. For us, "going somewhere" glossed over most of the problems.

We were going somewhere, that is, until we heard an abnormal clunk from the engine compartment followed by ominous banging.

"What do you suppose that was?" Dad asked the steering wheel. There certainly wouldn't have been any point in asking us.

"It sounds like the engine is falling out," said Sandy with a noticeable lack of surprise in her voice.

"I suppose I'd better take a quick peek." Dad reluctantly slowed us down from our top speed of fifteen miles an hour and pulled over to the side, so that we were only blocking three quarters of the road.

While the rest of us bushwhacked our way through the tall, chigger infested roadside grass in search of private bushes to piddle behind, Dad opened the hood and searched among the problems for one that might be recent and worse than the rest.

"I think we've broken one of the engine mounts," he finally shouted to our various bushes. The engineers who designed them apparently thought they were working on a car. This was more like a bucking bronco with an engine in it.

"What does that mean?" Mom asked

from behind a relatively ample bush. We were still a long way from Aguaytia, whose river had supplied the rocks that did us in. The dusty green jungle stretched flat and empty as far as our scratchy eyes could see. No auto parts stores, no rest areas, no nothing but thatched huts that didn't look as if they stocked engine mounts.

"Well, it means if another one breaks, the engine really could fall out," Dad said matter of factly. It sounded more serious than he sounded. "But there's nothing I can do about it here, so let's just keep going and pray that we make it to Aguaytia."

Since this whole car was an answer to our prayers, prayer was rapidly losing its luster. Still, it did seem that only a miracle would get us to a shop.

We had allowed some extra time for the trip in case of car trouble, but walking or hitchhiking the remaining 450 miles to Lima was out of the question. Aguaytia would be far short of our goal for the day, but at least we might find a welder there.

To our surprise, the remaining engine mount held fast through the final torturous hours. Slowly we gained altitude as we labored into the foothills of the Andes. The blazing red sun sank into the clay white dust, first giving our world a reddish glow and then reducing it to the two puny beams of light pointing out rocks, ruts, bumps, holes and animals in front of us. We went numb.

Finally a long concrete bridge over the rock quarry river announced our arrival in Aguaytia. It was our first smooth road since we'd left Yarinacocha twelve hours before. We wanted to drive back and forth, back and forth, back and forth, just to feel it. In the dimished noise, we could almost hear each other shouting.

Aguaytia had been the first jungle headquarters for our linguistics teams in Peru. The river was wide enough for float planes, though it took a bit of timing to get the plane up on step, under the bridge and off the water between rapids. The old headquarters itself was a huge wooden house on a hill overlooking the town and the river.

Unfortunately our co-workers had long since moved out and turned the house back over to the government agency that had loaned it to us. We didn't know a soul in Aguaytia.

"Where are we going to stay?" one of us finally wondered out loud. There were no hotels or guest houses in the little town, and it was already past ten o'clock. We were filthy and starved and exhausted. Mary and Joseph in a dying car. Fortunately no one was pregnant.

"Let's go ask at the old house," Dad suggested. It seemed like the only possibility, so he turned us off the main road and up the long steep rocky driveway to the top of the hill. He got out of the car and banged on the door until the caretaker woke up and opened it a crack.

"Is there any chance you'd have room for us to spend the night?"

"How many of you are there?"

"My wife and I and four children. Our car broke down and we have no place to stay."

It's hard to say what the caretaker thought he was seeing, but he didn't exactly fling the door open. Gringos weren't an everyday occurrence, especially in the middle of the night and looking as if they'd just been resurrected from the dust of the earth. On the other hand, Dad was making a pretty good case for mercy and compassion.

"Look at my wife and little children," he pointed. "They're really tired." His wife immediately slunk down behind the seat so she couldn't be seen and his children would not have reassured anyone. We were clearly desperate.

Undoubtedly against his better judgment, and probably because he didn't have a stable to offer, the caretaker let us into the otherwise vacant house. We sprawled like wounded soldiers on musty beds or floors and immediately were oblivious to our troubles.

Morning brought a splendid view of the river valley, a couple of boiled eggs apiece and a welder with two teeth and a torch. Broken engine mounts, missing mufflers, and cracked axles kept his tin shack business thriving. He was probably the only person around who hoped the road would never be paved. A dollar later he was done.

By the time the engine mount was repaired to local standards, which meant we might be returning soon, we had swallowed our slippery eggs and saltine crackers and washed our faces. Full baths, we hoped, would be a luxurious treat at the tourist hotel in Tingo Maria at the end of the day. Slow learners that we were, we still had hopes for a better life.

In high spirits we piled in, encouraged to note that we couldn't hear any loud banging over the normal rattling and clanging. All things considered, the car was back to normal, which was nothing to sing about but better than yesterday.

Once past Aguaytia the road wound steadily upward through luxurious jungle-covered mountains. Orchids hung from branches. Ferns of all sizes covered the cliffs above and below the road. The air cooled perceptibly.

Within a couple of hours we entered the Boqueron, a canyon of towering cliffs carved by a raging, roaring, cascading river. In our high school years this would become a favorite camping spot. But that's another story.

The road was literally chiseled out of the cliffs and was so narrow that trucks with dual tires in the back sometimes had one tire hanging over space. In our case, all four tires stayed squarely on the road, but Mom's constant gasps and white knuckled grip reminded us how close we all were to eternity. I still wonder why someone would hang on so tightly to something they were sure was on the verge of going over a cliff.

On one side of the car we could shamelessly pull four foot fern leaves off the canyon walls. On the other, we could launch them into space and watch them drift in giant lazy circles until they landed in the foaming waters of the river. If Mom had been watching the ferns instead of the precipice, her whole outlook would have been more peaceful.

There were two long tunnels in the canyon. Just before the first one, we lurched to a halt behind a stalled truck. The driver and his helper were both squatting beside the back tires.

"What's the problem?" Dad asked leaning his head out the window.

"It's too tall to go through the tunnel. We're letting some air out of the tires."

Since we couldn't get past it, we hopped out for some lunch, some fern flying and some rock throwing. It would take a while for the driver to let enough air out and then refill the tires on the other side.

In retrospect, this was probably the only part of the trip that we really enjoyed. Water cascaded down the sides of the canyons in waterfalls that ranged from angel hair mist to crashing torrents. Daily rains kept the whole canyon wet and luxuriously green. It even smelled green. Bright orange cock o' the rocks made their nests in the crevices. Huge blue morpho butterflies flopped their wings in erratic paths.

In the narrow window of sky above us, the sun worked to take the chill off the mountain air. The only sounds were the river, the waterfalls, and the air hissing slowly out of the tires in front of us.

Too soon all good things must come to an end. Before we wished, we were back in the car and winding our way up out of the canyon with horn blasts echoing off the walls at every turn. The narrow road and blind turns required advance notice that we were coming through and hopefully would keep us from getting pushed into the river by a drunken driver. They used to say that you had to be a little drunk to have the nerve to drive this section. Most were.

Dad's arms spun first one direction, then the other dodging holes and keeping us on the road. It wasn't long before we came across a truck with more than tire problems, judging from bits and pieces spread on the ground. By skinning a little paint off the car we could have gotten around, but the driver signalled us to stop.

"Can you give me a ride to Tingo Maria? My transmission is broken." The driver was short and dark and covered with grease and dust. He would feel right at home with us.

"Sure," said Dad, always eager to help and well aware that we ourselves might soon be in the driver's shoes. "Get in the back with the kids."

In midafternoon, climbing over a high pass, the windows were closed against the cold, trapping engine and body fumes. Body parts, both ours and the car's, bounced and rattled interminably. Road grime poured through unseen gaps and filled our pores.

Tight hairpin turns zig zagged us to the summit and then down the other side until finally, closing in on Tingo, we could see a straight stretch at the end of the canyon. The stomach churning curves were about to end. We had made it through the Boqueron and over the pass. Sighs of relief all around. Mom slackened her grip. Dad relaxed into the straightaway.

"Hey," Dad yelped as the car suddenly swerved to the right, directly for the roadside ditch. Then, "Oh no!" He whipped the steering wheel, but it was no longer connected to anything. Mom gasped and locked onto her door handle. Our passenger in the back jerked upright and crossed himself.

Only our slow speed and good brakes

saved us. We screeched to a halt in a narrow patch of grass between the road and the ditch, got out slowly and began our habitual search for private bushes while Dad once again crawled under the car.

Our passenger was jabbering as if he had just come through a death and resurrection.

"That was very lucky. This is a miracle. What would have happened if it had come loose back in the canyon? *Dios mio* we are very lucky. *Dios mio* this was a miracle. *Ay Dios mio* thank you for the good luck." And on and on in a heartfelt mixture of theology and lucky coincidence.

Having our steering linkage hold together until the first straight stretch of the day was surely an act of God, and we all knew enough to be very grateful. Still, we had to figure out how to get the rest of the way to Tingo. Driving without an engine mount is pretty tame compared to driving without steering.

Our dusty passenger saved us. Having spent his life fixing broken trucks in the middle of mountains and jungle, he immediately dived under the car.

"Do you have any wire or rope?" his muffled voice came from just in front of the muffler.

A quick search turned up nothing that could conceivably tie anything together.

"How about your belt," the muffled voice suggested to dad. It wasn't designed to hold steering linkages together, but this come-along stranger was an old hand at improvisation. He set right to work, winding and twisting with his bare hands. When he was done, everything turned when it was supposed to and didn't when it wasn't and we were off again, wondering just how durable the leather in the belt would be.

What with the tunnel and steering setbacks, we were once again hopelessly behind schedule, but we still made it to Tingo in the daylight.

In a rare fit of financial extravagance we headed straight for the Hotel Turista when we entered town at 4:30 in the afternoon. It wasn't exactly five star, but its rustic cabins stretched out along a beautiful stream and were surrounded by lush tropical plants.

When the doorman came to get our luggage, Mom hid behind the seat again. He was obviously trying to figure out how to carry our assorted boxes and bags without touching them. We spared him the dirty uniform by lifting them to our own shoulders and marching along behind his starched back.

Within minutes we were spread out wading in the freezing, shallow water, skipping rocks and soaking up the dwindling day. Within an hour the sun would set, cold would drop on us like a wet blanket and we would head for the bliss of a hot meal and bath.

In the end, of course, our hot meal was eaten with shaking spoons and there was no hot bath. The showers offered only freezing cold water in cement shower stalls. The whole picturesque place went frigid after six.

"I don't feel that dirty," volunteered Dad. "I think I'll just wash my face and go to bed. Mom followed without a murmur and the rest of us, having long since acclimated to the jungle's humid heat, decided on the spot that we felt cleaner than we'd originally thought. In no time we had tucked ourselves in against the worsening cold.

Some of us slept. Mom lay awake most of the night listening to the babbling stream, shivering and worrying about the rest of the trip. Her confidence in our ability to survive hadn't been greatly enhanced by the first two days.

CHAPTER 16

Tingo Maria to Lima

Dad woke us up wondering just what would break down next.

"I'm going to find someplace to get the car fixed. Eat breakfast and get your stuff packed so we can shove off as soon as I get back." 'Shove off' had to have been a throwback to Dad's life in the Navy, but it seemed rather appropriate for this car.

"Can't we stay here another day and play?" Melody begged. "I'm tired of riding in the car. Let's do something funner." She wasn't being specific, but almost anything would've been "funner" than getting back in the smelly car.

"They're working on the road right now, so we've got to get over the pass to Huanuco today while the traffic's going our direction. Otherwise we'll have to wait two more days." Dad didn't realize how appealing that sounded to the rest of us. Still, we were well behind schedule, so we would have to press on.

Dad wandered the streets of Tingo looking for someone with the right parts to fix our steering linkage. None of us particularly wanted to see how long his belt would last. We shivered through breakfast on the veranda and packed up our increasingly dirty gear.

In between bites and bags, we floated leaf boats in the the river.

"Come look at the sleeping lady," Mom urged us. With the help of our vivid imaginations, we stared up at her, a ridge of mountains that looked sort of like the face, bust, belly, knees and toes of a woman lying on her back. She looked blue with cold, but at least she was sleeping better than Mom had.

After the customary prayers for safety (obviously urgent), wisdom (we should've given this some thought before we said we'd take the car), and no more car breakdowns (a miracle, in other words) our day started out following a river much like the Boqueron in miniature. The steering linkage was working perfectly again.

Lush green cliffs crowded us against the dropoff beside us, but gave sensational views of white water cascading over a boulder strewn valley.

Once out of the river valley we climbed in earnest, spinning back and forth as we followed the switchbacks ever upward. If the rapture used this route, it would take years to get us all to heaven.

"Aren't the tea gardens beautiful? They're so green you just want to stare and stare." Mom was obviously sitting in the front seat. In the back seat, we were greener than the tea gardens and staring at plants was pretty low priority.

"You kids need to learn to appreciate this stuff," Dad tried. "Think how many kids never get a chance to do this." We thought all those unknown kids were particularly lucky today.

In many places the road was not only torn up from the construction, it was so steep that stopping might mean we couldn't get started again. Low clouds swirled around us, reducing visibility to a couple hundred feet and keeping the road and everything else damp and cold. It would be a terrible place to meet a stopped truck.

We met a stopped truck.

"What's wrong with it?" Melody asked as if the rest of us would somehow magically know.

"I think he's broken down," Sandy answered. Sandy would magically know most anything.

Fortunately the driver's helper had placed a rock behind each wheel to keep it from rolling back into our laps. Mom didn't think the rocks looked very secure, so she once again tightened her grip on her casket. The rest of us got out to stretch and to breathe uncontaminated air. Our breath blew out in white clouds.

"*Que paso?*" Dad asked a pair of dirty shoes sticking out from under the transmission.

"My clutch is slipping," came the Spanish answer from five feet in front of the shoes. "I'll have it adjusted *en un momentito.*" "*Momentito*" originally meant 'in a short moment.' Here in the mountains it could mean minutes or years.

Within less than a *momentito* our teeth chattered and our bodies shivered and our lips turned blue. We were only too happy to hear the truck engine roar back to life, coughing and backfiring while it cleared its throat.

"Climb aboard," Dad yelled. He clearly wanted us to be together as a family when the truck with its slipping clutch rolled over us. Nevertheless, aboard we climbed, warmed by the exaust fumes that gushed our way.

The driver raced his engine a dozen times, blasting us with more clouds of hot smoke. He let off the parking brake and the truck rolled perceptibly backwards against its rock chocks.

"Something's burning." Terry was the first to say it, but we all smelled the pungent smoke. It was by now unusual to smell anything but ourselves.

"It's his clutch," Dad answered. Through the haze that enveloped us we heard the gears growl angrily. The heat of the snarling engine washed over us and finally, heavily the truck crawled up the hill to a chorus of blue lipped cheers.

"Jump out and get those rocks out of the road," Dad ordered as he started our car and put it in gear. That would mean Terry and me, since we had bullied Sandy into the middle of the back seat.

We jumped as told, cleared the road and scrambled back in. Our car wasn't breathing too well in the thin air. Two of the eight cylinders had sore throats and coughed regularly. We all wondered just how we would manage the 16,000' pass if we could barely manage this 10,000' summit.

Still, we were moving in the right direction, and within a few kilometers passed the truck with the burnt clutch. The driver, in a rare fit of wisdom, had pulled over at a wide spot and called it quits, rocks again placed firmly behind each wheel.

Once over the summit, where we saw nothing but the cloud that surrounded us, it was a long downhill coast to Huanuco. Trucks used low gears and backfired as if they were shooting at each other. Going down was no faster than going up.

Huanuco. The day's ordeal was almost over. In minutes we would be at a nice hotel, finally able to eat and bathe.

Without notice, we all heard a loud banging and scraping at the front of the car, as if someone were cutting the engine out with a skill saw.

"Now what?" Mom asked in a voice that was ragged with exhaustion. Mom could never sleep in a car, and since she couldn't sleep too well in hotels either, this had been a long trip.

Dad pulled over, unfolded himself into the cold and lifted the hood.

"Our radiator fell out. The fan blade kind of chewed it up." At least it hadn't taken long to diagnose the problem this time. Steaming water spurted on the concrete bridge as our car bled to death.

This time we were at least within shouting distance of our hotel. We limped in, dejectedly ejected, and paid for rooms. Dressed and wrapped in anything that looked warm, the impression we gave was that six bales of used clothing had just arrived for recycling.

"What are we doing for supper?" The restaurant in the hotel was already closed and we were close to starvation.

"Let's go find some chicken," Dad suggested. Reluctantly we all dragged our bundled warmth stiffly back outside, hugging ourselves like forlorn orphans. The car, waterless now, at least got us to a warm supper and delivered us back to our tourist hotel.

"There's no hot water." Mom confirmed what we had all come to expect by now. "Let's just go to bed and bathe in the morning." In the mountain air, we could at least add layers of clothing on top of those that were starting to ferment underneath.

In the morning, of course, there still wasn't any hot water. Dad left on his solitary trek to find another radiator. The rest of us shivered and packed.

This day would make or break us. Everyone who knew anything about the road to Lima had given the same warning:

"Whatever you do, don't spend the night in Cerro de Pasco. If you stay there you'll get *seroche* and you'll freeze to death. There's no good place to stay there anyway — it's just a mining town."

Seroche was the dreaded altitude sickness that made heads pound and stomachs wrench. At 15,000 windswept, treeless feet above sea level, Cerro de Pasco was high on our list of miserable places to miss.

Of course you already know what's

coming. By the time Dad got back to report that the radiator had been at least temporarily soldered, we were well past our planned departure time. Prudence would have suggested laying over for a day. Prudence wasn't along on this trip. Off we went, coating ourselves with a fresh layer of dust and exhaust as we climbed higher into the Andes.

"Look at the llamas," Melody said from her privileged front seat position. "Aren't they pretty!" We all straightened from our slouches to see a colorfully decorated herd of them crowding the road in front of us, each carrying a small bundle. Behind the herd a Quechua man and his wife walk-trotted, their leathery faces and hands parched from cold lives in the mountains.

The wife's four or five multicolored skirts swayed rhythmically. As she loped along carrying her baby cocooned in a blanket on her back, she spun wool on a hand carved bobbin.

Throughout the day we would see more llamas, sheep, alpacas and goats, not that they would do us any good. The travel bingo cards that a friend in the U.S. had sent us didn't include llamas and alpacas.

Throughout the day's climb our engine

griped and complained. Powerless without oxygen, it barely kept us moving. At one particularly steep climb somewhere around 14,000 feet, it finally refused to go a foot further, succumbing to *seroche* even before we did.

The road was so steep that it would have been a challenge in the low lands. Up here we were totally stuck. We would all have gotten out and pushed, but in the thin air we had no more energy or strength than the car.

Several times we backed down the slope to a slightly more level spot and raced forward, engine sputtering and tires spinning in the loose gravel. Every time the result was the same — a pathetic whimpering whine and engine failure.

About to give up, Dad finally had an inspiration.

"Let's try it backwards. I think the gearing is lower in reverse." His Model T days had included similar tactics on steep hills.

It was no small feat getting the car turned around in the narrow road, but when we finally had, the result was a screaming, rattling, clutch riding, weaving backward ascent. Sir Edmund Hillary couldn't have been more elated.

By evening, *seroche* and car sickness were pounding us. Dad had no relief driver. The landscape was bleak and barren. A freezing wind rocked the car. All warnings aside, we would have to spend the night in Cerro de Pasco.

"I'll see if they'll let us stay at the mining company's guest house," Dad moaned. "Maybe they'll take pity on us." They didn't normally let anyone stay in the guest house but employees.

He returned gray and tired and shaking with cold and exhaustion.

"They said we can have one room. We can only put four of us in it, so you two will have to sleep in the car." He was looking at Terry and me, and we reluctantly resigned ourselves to a night in the freezer.

With no appetite for supper, and none available anyway, we all covered ourselves with every available fabric and tried to sleep away the headaches and dizziness.

Terry and I were roughly wakened by a blast of cold air at three in the morning. It was Dad, carrying Melody.

"Scoot over so Sandy and Melody can get in. If I don't get out of here now, I'm afraid I won't be able to drive." We scooted, they piled and miraculously the car started.

Not for long. By the time we'd reached the remote outskirts of Cerro, a brilliant red warning light told us that the car was overheating, of all things. It had to be the only overheated thing within two hundred kilometers.

Dad hurried to open the hood, blue faced and panting at the exertion of just getting to the front of the car. The radiator, of course, was frozen. An overheated engine right behind a frozen radiator. Life is full of ironies.

If ever we were desperate, now was the time. A rapidly deteriorating driver. An already deteriorated car. Artic air without oxygen. We were all silent, wondering what would happen to us.

"Give me a flashlight," Dad ordered through clenched teeth. "I've got to find some water to pour over the radiator." It was amazing that the beam from the flashlight didn't get blown away by the wind as he searched the sides of the road.

"Hey, there's a faucet here! Get me a pan." With no pan readily available, our little enamel potty would have to do. He turned on the faucett. In a moment of pure compassion, God had kept the water from freezing in the pipe when it froze in our radiator.

A couple dozen trips and dumps were all it took to thaw the radiator and freeze Dad's hands. He lept in and we roared off with a fresh understanding of God's special provision.

By the time the sun came up we listed rather badly to starboard. A spring shackle had broken in the pre-dawn blackness, surrounding us with a loud and bumpy banging. When daylight finally came we could pull into a house turned junk yard beside the road.

One look at the odd assortment of long dead cars and trucks left no doubt that we would find nothing to match our American import. Still, Dad climbed out.

"Do you have a spring shackle that would fit this car?" he asked the puzzled, rosy cheeked old man in the bright yarn pullover.

The bright pullover disappeared into the heaps, returning moments later with a huge smile and just what we needed. He handed it to his son and explained to Dad that he wanted his son to get some mechanical experience. We weren't as thrilled as he was at his son's unexpected opportunity to learn a new trade.

When the son hadn't made any visible progress in an hour, Dad could wait no longer.

"Here's fifty soles," he said, feeling quite generous at giving the failing son $3.30. "I'll finish putting it on." By the time we drove away, everyone was happy: the other father because his son had learned something, the son because he'd gotten paid for doing nothing, and our father because we had just found the right spring shackle in the middle of nowhere. We could be on our sprung way once again.

The rest of the trip was an altitude induced blur. We took turns vomiting out the windows or into the potty. We could barely appreciate the asphalt road that signalled our three hour descent into Lima, especially since it speeded up the never ending switchbacks and increased the car sickness. When we finally pulled up at our group's guest house we felt like refugees just back from a week's foraging at the town dump.

Someone swung open the double doors that would let us into the interior parking area. It took a few moments to realize that it was over. For five days we had averaged ten miles an hour. We hadn't bathed the whole trip. Our lips were chapped, the sides of our mouths and the sides of the car covered with dried vomit. The air inside was thick with fumes and smells from us and the overflowing potty. Somewhere along the way we had given up on emptying it.

"Welcome to Lima House," the cheerful, clean voice outside the car said. "We were beginning to wonder what had happened to you. Did you have a good trip?"

Bleak gray-green stares all around. No answers.

Finally, coming to our senses, we tried to get out. My door, the back right, wouldn't open. Terry's, the back left, was equally stuck shut. Mom's, the front right, didn't budge. And so we exited, for the last time, all climbing over the seats, scooching past the steering wheel and tumbling through the driver's door. We never set foot in the car again — a gracious answer to our prayers.

EPILOGUE

Our first ten years in the jungle weren't exactly boring. But we really put our guardian angels through their paces during my high school years. By then we were old enough to have some real fun.

That's when I got my horse that screeched to a halt every time I urged her to go faster … and when I built the huge go-cart that we couldn't steer … and paddled down the Urubama and Ucayali with a friend in an overloaded dugout canoe for two weeks … and spent five weeks in a totally isolated little village surviving on manioc roots and building a useless airstrip.

Of course I'll never forget the time our car broke down in the middle of a landslide on the edge of a cliff, and we raced to see if we could dig it out of the mud before the road eroded right out from under us.

… But that's another book.

Global EncounTours

How would you like to visit Peru? How about an adventure to Machiguenga-land with Rani Snell? Sound like fun?

If it does, Ron's wife, Esther, founded Global EncounTours for folks just like you — folks who want to travel, but don't want to go as a "tourist." Each tour is conducted by someone who has "been there, done that and is itching to do it again."

Tours range from "Comfortable With a Light Sprinkling of Adventure" to "Rani's Idea of an Adventure." We do promise no one will have to ride a log without a paddle, and we'll even show you which end of the paddle is the handle.

Our excursions are well planned, but since some of the funnest, funniest and most touching experiences aren't always on the itinerary, we specialize in taking full advantage of serendipitous happenings.

Still sound like fun? If you are interested in joining a scheduled tour or having us tailor-make a tour for your group, contact Esther at Global EncounTours: 534 Park Lane, Duncanville, TX 75116. Phone 214-296-5470, Fax 214-709-8848 or e-mail EncounTour@AOL.COM

Please send me:

"It's a Jungle Out There!" by Ron Snell.

_____ Copies at $5.95 = _____

On the 8th Day... God Laughed! by Gene Perret with Terry Perret Martin. 900 jokes arranged alphabetically by topic. Humor that tickles your funnybone while it honors the Creator.

_____ Copies at $5.95 = _____

Way Back in the Kornfields, by James C. Hefley. 900 jokes that will make Grandpa laugh without making Grandma blush.

_____ Copies at $5.95 = _____

Way Back in the Ozarks, by Howard Jean Hefley & James C. Hefley. Hilarious, heartwarming true stories of a boy named "Monk," his dog & his coon.

_____ Copies at $5.95 = _____

Ozark Mountain Hymns, Audio cassette tape features banjo, fiddle, dobro mandolin & acoustic guitar. New songs & old time favorites.

_____ Tapes at $6.95 = _____

Please add $2.00 postage and handling for first book, plus .50 for each additional book.

Shipping & Handling _____

MO residents add sales tax _____

TOTAL ENCLOSED
(Check or money order)_____

Name _____

Address _____

City _____ State____ Zip _____